MY LIFE'S JOURNEY

ALTAF HUSSAIN

MY LIFE'S JOURNEY

The Early Years (1966–1988)

A translation of
SAFAR-E-ZINDAGI

Original Urdu Version Compiled by
KHALID ATHAR

Foreword by
MATTHEW A. COOK

Introductions by
ROBERT NICHOLS
BRIGADIER A.R. SIDDIQI

OXFORD
UNIVERSITY PRESS

OXFORD

UNIVERSITY PRESS

No. 38, Sector 15, Korangi Industrial Area, PO Box 8214,
Karachi-74900, Pakistan

Oxford University Press is a department of the University of Oxford.
It furthers the University's objective of excellence in research, scholarship,
and education by publishing worldwide in

Oxford New York

Auckland Cape Town Dar es Salaam Hong Kong Karachi
Kuala Lumpur Madrid Melbourne Mexico City Nairobi
New Delhi Shanghai Taipei Toronto

With offices in

Argentina Austria Brazil Chile Czech Republic France Greece
Guatemala Hungary Italy Japan Poland Portugal Singapore
South Korea Switzerland Turkey Ukraine Vietnam

Oxford is a registered trademark of Oxford University Press
in the UK and in certain other countries

Published in Pakistan by Oxford University Press, Karachi

Typeset in Cambria
Printed in Pakistan by
Kagzi Printers, Karachi.
Published by
Ameena Saiyid, Oxford University Press
No. 38, Sector 15, Korangi Industrial Area, PO Box 8214,
Karachi-74900, Pakistan.

Dedicated
to
The People of Pakistan

Contents

Safar-e-Zindagi
(A note from the publisher of the original, Urdu work)

Safar-e-Zindagi is based on a lengthy interview, extended over a period of time, which Mr Altaf Hussain, founder and leader of the MQM, accorded to the journalist Khalid Athar. It was first published in the leading Urdu daily, *Jang*. Now it is being presented in book form to apprise readers of the early struggle of the MQM and its leader's philosophy and views.

Foreword

Mohajirs, Sindh, and Pakistan

Mohajir Quami Movement (MQM) and its founder Altaf Hussain are examples of the truism that people and their institutions are the products of particular histories. Founded in 1984 to represent post-Partition immigrants from India, the MQM (now called the Muttahida Quami Movement) draws its strongest support from Urdu-speakers in the Sindh region of Pakistan.[1] Originally from various locales (e.g., Uttar Pradesh, Andhra Pradesh, Delhi, Rajasthan, and Bombay), these immigrants—*mohajirs*—originated from Muslim minority locations in India.[2]

Many mohajirs migrated to Pakistan with the perception of 'themselves as the embodiment of this new state'.[3] Accordingly, as Sarah Ansari writes in *Life after Partition*, they attempted to 'reproduce or replicate within their new homes the kinds of "boundaries" which had delineated their communities in the past'.[4] When combined with the idea of Pakistan as a historical movement that 'transcended the structures of power and everyday life that shaped the territories that in fact came to comprise the country', this outlook resulted in mohajirs advocating that they—as much as the Muslim communities already living in the Indus River region—were 'natives'.[5] Bolstered by a large number of post-

Partition immigrants, this thinking had a transformative impact on Sindh—particularly its urban demographics.[6] By 1960, less than 20 per cent of the region's main city, Karachi, was Sindhi. By 1990, 50 per cent of the people in Karachi (i.e., six million) as well as Sindh's second city of Hyderabad (i.e., one million) were mohajirs.[7] In light of such demographics, mohajirs not only sought to maintain pre-Partition influence over national-level politics but develop a greater regional voice in the affairs of Sindh. For example, they argued that mohajirs should occupy legislative assembly seats vacated by those who migrated to India.

Mohajirs (as a result of sacrificing their homes and wealth for the nation) were initially and popularly viewed as intellectual leaders in Pakistan.[8] Nonetheless, most mohajirs were not elites. Working-class mohajirs—e.g., artisans like shoemakers and carpet weavers from Agra, metal workers from Moradabad, lock-makers from Aligarh, etc.—found economic adjustment to life in Pakistan difficult. Establishing a more secure economic footing was thus a high priority for them. However, from their perspective, Sindhis stymied this priority by acquiring large amounts of property owned by individuals who left Pakistan for India.[9] There was thus a 'mismatch' between what immigrants wanted and what Sindhis controlled. The fact that Sindhis—in contrast to mohajirs—were predominately rural helped exacerbate resentment about this mismatch. The politics of this mismatch often did not favour immigrants, who were not adequately organized after Partition to challenge Sindh's established interests. The region's local politicians were also not as sensitive to mohajir claims as they could have been: most provincial refugee rehabilitation ministers were Sindhis rather than mohajirs.[10] By the beginning of the 1950s, Sindh's rural population which, in overall terms, was six times the size of that found in its towns and cities, fed this power differential, despite the increasing urban influence of mohajirs.[11] As a result, Ansari concludes: 'Throughout this period, community distinctions continued to harden'.[12] These distinctions were further aggravated by neither group dominating certain key political-economic niches: Karachi's civil and police administrations were heavily controlled by Punjabis, while this community—along with Pakhtuns—also dominated the building and transportation sectors.[13] The overall effect was to 'increase Sindhi concerns at what they perceived to be their deteriorating position within their own province, while presenting other refugee communities with their own sources of grievance'.[14]

Military rule in Pakistan, starting from 1958, did not diminish divisions between mohajirs and Sindhis. Immigrants initially supported military rule: General Ayub Khan's 'Clean Up the Mess' campaign pinpointed mohajir resettlement as a key issue. While martial law did speed up resettlements, it also more firmly established the military—an institution dominated by Punjabis—in Sindh. Aiming to consolidate their control, martial law authorities announced land reforms to undermine the influence of rural Sindhi landowners. Due to these authorities' strong Punjabi connections, Ansari writes:

> Indeed, many *zamindars* [i.e., agricultural landlords] in Sindh subscribed to the belief that land reform was nothing but a device to permit more Punjabi cultivators to acquire land in their province.[15]

The shift of Pakistan's capital from Karachi to the Punjabi cities of Rawalpindi (in 1958) and Islamabad (in 1960) was also a source of concern for the Sindhis. This shift additionally threatened the influence of mohajirs, who were well-represented in Pakistan's Karachi-based bureaucracy following Partition.[16] Ayub Khan's drive to eradicate corruption among state workers compounded this threat. Despite their initial support, the military rule of Pakistan under Ayub Khan (1958–1969) and then Yahya Khan (1969–1971) did not excessively benefit mohajirs. Instead, it signalled an alienation from the corridors of power as provincial rivalries increasingly favoured Punjabis with military connections. Nonetheless, since the military's centralization of power benefited their resettlement so directly, mohajirs remained the target of criticism by provincial politicians in Sindh.

Bangladesh's independence following the 1971 war between Pakistan and India was a crisis that exacerbated differences between mohajirs and Sindhis. Bangladesh's independence challenged Pakistan's ideological existence as a homeland for South Asian Muslims. One response, writes Stephen Cohen in *The Idea of Pakistan*, was to shift toward a greater ideological commitment to Islam.[17] Another was to valorise 'primordial ethnic distinctions as constitutive of the overall nation'.[18] Zulfikar Ali Bhutto's Pakistan People's Party (PPP), with its support base in rural Sindh, advocated this approach during its rule of Pakistan from 1971 to 1977. The approach affirmed Pakistan's indigenous ethnicities, particularly rural Sindhis. It also marginalized those without ethnic roots in the national soil, like urban mohajirs.[19] This marginalization was so great that Oskar Verkaaik, in *The Sufi Saints of Sindhi Nationalism*, bluntly concludes: 'The Sindhi revival in the 1970s under the rule of the Pakistan People's Party was not favourable for them [i.e., mohajirs]'.[20]

In response to the 'Sindhi revival', mohajirs declared themselves a *qaum* or ethnic group.[21] They argued—as Altaf Hussain does in *My Life's Journey*—that mohajirs were ethnically equal to other Pakistanis and thus deserved similar treatment (e.g., as a reserved category in higher education admissions). The declaration by Hussain that mohajirs were a *qaum* represents a significant shift in Pakistan's political history. Before and after Partition mohajirs supported Pakistan's founding political party, the Muslim League. However, the inability of the Muslim League to adequately address immigrant resettlement alienated mohajirs. In contrast, the Islamic party Jamaat-e-Islami positively impacted immigrant assistance in post-Partition Pakistan. Mohajirs subsequently shifted support from the Muslim League to

Jamaat-e-Islami in the 1950s.[22] Driven by the party's anti-ethnic politics and an Islamic nationalism that reaffirmed Pakistan's existence, this support continued into the 1980s. Verkaaik, in *Migrants and Militants*, describes how Hussain's founding of the All-Pakistan Mohajir Student Organization (APMSO) in 1978 and the MQM in 1984 shifted immigrant support away from Jamaat-e-Islami.[23] Its reaction to this shift (as well as the mohajir claim to be a *qaum*) was violent. Graphically described in *My Life's Journey*, this violence—in combination with its support in 1977 for a 'Punjabi' and 'Islamic' military coup by General Ziaul Haq—further antagonized mohajirs from Jamaat-e-Islami. Despite violence, the MQM gained popularity to become a major political party in Pakistan.

While violence does not hinder the MQM's popularity, it does further spoil the mohajir-Sindhi relationship during the 1980s. Verkaaik describes this period of Pakistan's politics as 'apocalyptic' due to its widespread vandalism, looting, extortion, blackmail, arson, torture and political assassination. He states: 'Many mohajirs sincerely believed they were on the verge of a final battle in which either they or their enemies would be exterminated'.[24] Such apocalyptic sentiment—when fed by the actions of rival ethnic groups—leads to increasing violence. The Hyderabad riots of 1990 result in an ethnically divided city among Sindhis and mohajirs. Verkaaik observes that this conflict later shifts to Karachi where 'more than two thousand people were killed in ambushes, bomb blasts and shootings'.[25] In Karachi, differences between Sindhis and mohajirs boil over to include other ethnic groups (e.g., Baloch, Pashtuns and Punjabis).[26] In 1992, Prime Minister Nawaz Sharif—whose own ethnic political base is in the Punjab—squashed Sindh-based ethnic conflict with military, paramilitary and intra-Pakistan intelligence personnel. A major outcome of 'Operation Clean-Up', which is partially based on the false claim that the MQM wants a separate homeland within Pakistan (i.e., Jinnahpur), is Altaf Hussain's exile to London. Even with this exile, violence continues: strife in Karachi killed over one thousand in 1994 and over two thousand in 1995.[27] Factionalism involving mohajirs killed more than seven hundred in 1998.[28] With many MQM members in hiding or in exile, mohajir-related violence subsequently dropped. Nonetheless, killing of prominent MQM members represents the potential for violence to again burn in Pakistan. For example, the situation in Karachi was extremely tense after the murder of Imran Farooq, Convener of the MQM, on 16 September 2010 in London (a colleague of Altaf Hussain and one of the founding members of the MQM who was living in exile).[29]

Particular histories—like that of the mohajirs—seem to indicate that nationalism is a failed project in Pakistan. Since its citizens are not historically cemented into a more singular nation, group distinctions (arising from Partition) continue to define everyday Pakistani lives. This is particularly the case in Sindh. Ansari concludes:

In many ways, by the end of the twentieth century, therefore, life in Sindh replicated that of the years following Partition, with boundaries between communities as, if not more, sharply delineated.[30]

Ansari is not alone in the sentiment that nationalism is not delivering its full potential to the citizens of Pakistan. Altaf Hussain adopts a similar position when he declares that the 'partition of the subcontinent was the biggest blunder in the history of mankind'.[31]

Nonetheless, due to its complex and variegated history, nationalism in Pakistan is better characterized by crisis rather than failure. Naveeda Khan, in *Beyond Crisis: Re-evaluating Pakistan*, maintains that this crisis is one of nationalism as self-contained 'sameness'.[32] She argues that it is a common alienation from this 'sameness' that binds Pakistanis together as a nation. This position views nationalism as an on-going dialectic that cannot operate outside of Pakistan's differences, like those based on ethnicity. These differences are not alien to Pakistani nationalism but continually constitute it through negation.[33] Violence between the MQM and Pakistani national forces during and after Operation Clean-up seemingly illustrates this negation.

This principle of negation also appears to drive tensions between mohajirs and Sindhis from one historical crisis to another. Nonetheless, while these crises are often anti-Sindhi, mohajir politics not only illustrates how negation produces alterity but—by opening socio-political conversations—the possibility of mimesis.[34] Verkaaik observes that MQM imagery of Altaf Hussain mimics Sindhi practices.[35] Its suspicion of domination by 'fundamentalists' and 'Punjabis' also mirrors existing Sindhi concerns. Reflecting mimetic possibilities, Verkaaik states: 'While the Sindhi ethnic movement has not won independence for Sindh, it has gained recognition even by one of its main opponents [i.e., the MQM]'.[36] Recent electoral alliances between mohajirs and Sindhis (i.e., the MQM and PPP) suggest that these possibilities can turn principles of identifying and/or distancing one group with/from another into positive alliances rather than negative conflicts.[37] They additionally illustrate how historical tensions between mohajirs and Sindhis are 'not conflicts to be resolved, but frameworks for the never ending negotiations that sustain community'.[38] Rather than negate socio-political life in Pakistan, such negotiations—through mimesis and alterity—historically constitute it.[39] In this sense, mohajir-Sindhi ethnic differences not only hold the potential for violent tension but a shared conversation, something that Pakistan needs more of if it is to fully deliver on its possibilities as a nation.

Matthew A. Cook
Assistant Professor
Postcolonial and South Asian Studies
History and English Departments
North Carolina Central University
Durham
North Carolina
USA

Notes

1. The MQM's somewhat ironic exchange of mohajir for *muttahida* (i.e., united) occurred in 1997.

2. The term mohajir derives from the same root as *hajji* or one who goes out on a holy pilgrimage.

3. Sarah Ansari, *Life after Partition: Migration, Community and Strife in Sindh, 1947–1962* (Karachi: Oxford University Press, 2005), p. 215.

4. Ibid., p. 11.

5. David Gilmartin, 'Living the Tensions of the State, the National and Everyday Life', in Naveeda Khan (ed.), *Beyond Crisis: Re-evaluation Pakistan* (London: Routledge, 2010), p. 522.

6. The mohajir impact in post-Partition Punjab was less contentious—in part—since many immigrants shared a common Punjabi ethnicity.

7. Oskar Verkaaik, *Migrants and Militants: 'Fun' and Urban Violence in Pakistan* (Princeton: Princeton University Press, 2004), p. 2.

8. Charles Lindholm, 'Three Styles in the Study of Violence', *Reviews in Anthropology* 37.1: 75

9. Ansari, p. 89; Vazira Fazila-Yacoobali Zamindar, *The Long Partition and the Making of Modern South Asia: Refugees, Boundaries and Histories* (New York: Columbia University Press, 2007), pp. 45–76.

10. Ansari, pp. 102–103.

11. Ibid., p. 75.

12. Ibid., p. 165.

13. Rabia Ahmed Specht, *Urbanization in Pakistan: The Case of Karachi* (Copenhagen: School of Architecture, 1983); Arif Hasan, Muhammad Younus, and S. Akbar Zaidi, *Understanding Karachi: Planning and Reform for the Future* (Karachi: City Press, 1999).

14. Ansari, p. 210.

15. Ibid., p. 195.

16. The MQM's agenda also included detaching Karachi from Sindh, but as a move to acknowledge its mohajir identity.

17. Stephen Cohen, *The Idea of Pakistan* (Washington, D.C.: The Brookings Institute, 2006).
18. Lindholm, p. 76
19. Oskar Verkaaik, 'The Sufi Saints of Sindhi Nationalism', in Michel Boivin and Matthew A. Cook (eds.), *Interpreting the Sindhi World: Essays on Society and History* (Karachi: Oxford University Press, 2010), p. 213.
20. Ibid.
21. Verkaaik, *Migrants and Militants*, p. 2.
22. Ansari, pp. 177–78.
23. Verkaaik, *Migrants and Militants*, p. 2.
24. Lindholm, p. 78.
25. Verkaaik, *Migrants and Militants*, p. 16.
26. Ansari, p. 212.
27. Moonis Ahmar, 'Ethnicity and State Power in Pakistan: The Karachi Crisis', *Asian Survey* 36.10 (1996): 1035.
28. Ansari, p. 213.
29. Imran Farooq was a significant figure in the MQM. So much so that he authors a short preface to *My Life's Journey* titled 'An Important Clarification'.
30. Ansari, p. 213.
31. Ibid., p. 220.
32. Naveeda Khan (ed.), *Beyond Crisis: Re-evaluation Pakistan* (London: Routledge, 2010), p. 15.
33. Humeira Iqtidar makes a similar argument regarding secular and fundamentalist politics in Pakistan (Humeira Iqtidar, *Secularism in Pakistan: A Failed Experiment* [Chicago: University of Chicago Press, 2011].)
34. Michael Taussig, *Mimesis and Alterity: A Particular History of the Senses* (London: Routledge, 1993).
35. Verkaaik, 'The Sufi Saints', p. 214.
36. Ibid.
37. The MQM and the PPP also align in 1988. Altaf Hussain's positive comments in *My Life's Journey* about G.M. Syed (the Sindhi

nationalist) reflect this alliance. However, this alliance only lasts until 1989.

38. Gilmartin, p. 523.
39. Ibid.

Preface

I was born in Karachi on 17 September 1953. My paternal grandfather, Maulana Mufti Ramzan Hussain, was the Mufti of Agra and a highly learned man. My maternal grandfather too, was an erudite theologian. My father, Nazir Hussain, was a station master in India. After he migrated to Pakistan, he worked in the office of a mill in Karachi. He died on 13 March 1967. My mother died nearly twenty years later, on 5 December 1985. We are seven brothers, five are older than me and one is younger. All my brothers are married. My family lived in a small house, built on 120 square yards, in Federal B Area, Karachi. My favourite attire was, and still is, *kurta, pyjama*, and a waistcoat.

I studied at the Government Boys Secondary School, Karachi, on Jail Road and, after taking my Matriculation examination in 1969, joined City College, Karachi, where I studied till the Intermediate level (Science). Between 1970–1971, the National Cadet Service Scheme attracted my attention through which I received a year's military training in Sindh and Balochistan as a member of the 57 Baloch Regiment. In 1974, after doing my B.Sc. from Islamia Science College and B. Pharmacy from the University of Karachi, I joined M. Pharmacy but was obliged to leave the university owing to some unavoidable circumstances.

After working at Seventh Day Adventist Hospital in Karachi as a trainee, and employment in a Pakistani and then in a multinational pharmaceutical company, I left to join my brother in the USA. I stayed in America for eighteen months and returned to Pakistan.

Earlier, as a student of the University of Karachi, I founded the All Pakistan Mohajir Students' Organization (APMSO) on 11 June 1978. Before that, in 1977, I had participated actively as a worker in the Nizam-e-Mustafa Movement of the Pakistan National Alliance (PNA) and was the President and General Secretary of the Students' Action Committee of the PNA. On 18 March 1984 I established the Mohajir Quami Movement known as the MQM.

So far I have been arrested three times in my life. The first time was on 14 August 1979 when I was leading a demonstration at the mausoleum of Quaid-i-Azam Mohammad Ali Jinnah for bringing the Mohajirs stranded in Bangladesh to Pakistan. On 2 October 1979 the Military Court sentenced me to nine months imprisonment with hard labour and five lashes. Thereafter I had to spend nine months with hard labour in Karachi's Central Jail. However, the High Court intervened to revoke the lashes.

I was arrested a second time on 31 October 1986 at Ghaggar Phatak when, after a historic meeting of the

MQM in Hyderabad, I was on my way back to Karachi via Thatta.

The last time I was put under detention was on 30 August 1987. On this occasion I courted arrest since the police were raiding the homes of MQM workers and harassing their families. Many cases were brought against me one of which was for allegedly stealing a policeman's hat. After the MQM's record victory in the Sindh Municipal elections, the government offered to release me on bail but I rejected their proposal. Consequently, in January 1988, all charges against me and all office bearers, workers and sympathizers of the MQM were dropped unconditionally.

The success which God has granted me in my rise in the politics of Sindh is actually the result of the cooperation I received from my colleagues and the prayers of my elders. Moreover, the affection and honour accorded to me by the middle classes and the poor of urban Sindh are also due to the magnanimity of God. Some people think that I attained this position overnight but the truth is that behind my present standing lies a long story of a hard struggle.

Altaf Hussain
1988

Introduction

In 1988 the Urdu newspaper, *Jang*, published an extended interview with Altaf Hussain, the leader of a rising political party, the Mohajir Quami Movement (MQM). The interview was conducted by the journalist, Khalid Athar, and published under the title *Safar-e-Zindagi* (Life's Journey). The text was significant because the interview and publication marked the emergence of a new and major political movement, one that self-consciously identified and represented a 'fifth nationality' in Pakistan, the Mohajirs. Mohajirs were the families and descendants of Urdu-speaking Muslims who had arrived largely in the urban areas of Sindh province after the partition of British India in 1947. In November 1987, voters rallied to this political identity and the MQM won local bodies elections in Karachi and Hyderabad. In the 1988 National Assembly elections the MQM won thirteen seats and became a major presence on the national stage.

In the *Jang* interview Altaf Hussain detailed the long years of struggle he and his core followers endured during the establishment of their movement. Prominent personalities and events from party history find their place in this text that is part autobiography and part political manifesto. The chapters that follow in the book are the English translation of this original Urdu journalism. The current publication might also be seen as marking a moment of transition for a political movement that, since 1997, has aspired to represent a national political constituency of the poor and disenfranchised, a shift symbolized by revising the party name to the Muttahida Quami Movement. Significant or not, in November 2009, an MQM candidate won a seat in the Gilgit-Baltistan Legislative Assembly. In 2010, an MQM member of the Azad Jammu and Kashmir Legislative Assembly served as minister in the AJK government.

The Mohajir Quami Movement was founded in 1984. It evolved from Altaf Hussain's experience as a life-long resident of Karachi (born in 1953), a young military recruit, a student leader, and a political activist in the 1970s. In the *Jang* interview Altaf Hussain described his political education as a personal realization of the failure of the original national vision of Pakistan. Rather than living in a land of equal opportunity for citizens unified by a common Muslim religion and culture, he noted his awakening to the reality that, since 1947, government institutions and political parties had organized themselves to serve only regional and ethnic interests. This was increasingly to the political and economic detriment of the many educated, middle class Mohajirs who had played a prominent role in the pre-1947 Pakistan movement and in the initial leadership of an independent Pakistan.

After suffering the traumas of leaving their homes and the relocations of 1947, 6.3 million Mohajirs out of a total of 33.7 million settled in West Pakistan. In 1951, the population of Karachi, the capital city, was 1.1 million. Fifty-eight per cent spoke Urdu, while only 14 per cent spoke Sindhi. Yet the untimely deaths of the first founder leaders, Mohammad Ali Jinnah in 1948, followed by the assassination of Liaquat Ali Khan in 1951, led to the decline of the Muslim League party and political turmoil in the new country. From the time that Ayub Khan, a Pakhtun general-autocrat, took over the reins of the country and moved its capital to Islamabad, Mohajirs' access to political power and government employment began a long process of decline. By the 1970s, the Zulfikar Ali Bhutto government was favouring the Sindhi language. Moreover, a quota system was introduced by him that restricted educational opportunities and official recruitments of the Mohajirs.

My Life's Journey documents a claim for a particular social identity and political authority. In Pakistan such claims have often been made at much too high a cost. Altaf Hussain has described his efforts as a student leader, and the founding of the All-Pakistan Mohajir Students' Organization (APMSO) in 1978. He was an advocate for community admissions to universities and equal access to facilities, including student hostels. The intense and often violent competition that occurred between student groups on Karachi's campuses taught the young activist permanent lessons about mobilizing party activists and street power.

My Life's Journey is presented here with the sub-title 'The Early Years (1966–1988)' and in two sections. Part I: 'The Struggle and Birth of the MQM' is Altaf Hussain's autobiographical portrayal of an emerging political consciousness of Mohajir identity. His early life as a military recruit and student included incidents of discrimination. He noticed those who were excluded were primarily those who were firstly, not 'sons of the soil' and secondly, who were not connected to elite networks of privilege and wealth. His personal tale reflected the post-1947 reality that Urdu-speaking migrants who had settled in Pakistan expecting to maintain or attain positions of high social, political, and economic status found they were increasingly shut out of networks of power and patronage.

Part II: 'Notes on Important Issues and the Mohajir Movement' is an outline of the many policy positions taken by Altaf Hussain and the MQM by the end of the 1980s. He states his position on Sindhi nationalism, including the political leader G.M. Syed. He addresses health-care and education, the Kalabagh Dam proposal, quotas, the local police forces, and his personal life. He also narrates the violence that his party members experienced as they claimed political access. Public gatherings and processions suffered attacks. Many were killed. Violence was endemic.

After the 1979 Soviet Union invasion of Afghanistan, millions of Afghan refugees resettled in Pakistan. Hundreds of thousands moved to Karachi where they competed for housing, jobs, and resources. From the 1980s, armed clashes involved ethnic, political, and criminal groups, often in opposition to police and paramilitary authorities. Violence became a constant dynamic of Karachi, fuelled by the trade in guns and drugs and by partisan clashes. Clashes also began to occur between provincial and national governments in their attempts to control the volatile situation in the metropolis.

My Life's Journey was produced to document and publicize the dramatic rise of a new political vision. It was meant to assert legitimacy for a party and leader ready to influence provincial and national politics. The narrative presented in 1988 only hints at the complex history that would follow for the MQM over the next decades. Political polarization, street violence, and the failure of provincial or national authorities to find political solutions led to military and Ranger interventions in Karachi in the 1990s. Under threat, Altaf Hussain left for London in 1991 on a permanent political exile. Since then, there has been a continuing inability of the multiple contending interests to renounce violence for political compromise and accommodation. Reminiscing about his student days, Altaf Hussain recalled how he and Azeem Tariq would accompany teams of students as they went from market to market collecting donations for the new organization. The violence of those years resulted in the death of Azeem Tariq who was killed in 1993.

This volume also includes 'An Important Clarification' written by late Dr Imran Farooq, a long-time Convener of the MQM. After the 1992 military operation in Karachi Dr Farooq spent seven years in hiding in Pakistan before fleeing to Britain. Another exile, he was murdered there in September 2010.

Robert Nichols
Associate Professor of History
Richard Stockton College of New Jersey
Pomona
New Jersey
USA

Introduction

Prelude to an Odyssey[1]

My Life's Journey is just a prelude to a heroic, Homeric Odyssey of the founder and leader of Muttahida Quami Movement (MQM) Altaf Hussain alias Altaf Bhai. The final destination—call it Destiny if you will—is the recreation of Jinnah's Pakistan where 'religion has nothing to do with the business of the state'.

This was the raison d'être of the Quaid's Pakistan based on equality, justice, and fair play for all, irrespective of 'one's personal faith'. That was the Quaid's dream, the moving spirit behind the creation of a country untainted by religious discrimination and bigotry. Call it secular or un-Islamic; there is no reversing the language or denying the substance of the Quaid's message.

Altaf Hussain clings steadfastly to the Quaid's concept of religion having nothing to do with the opportunistic and essentially amoral business of the state. All state-craft, all diplomacy would be the law of the jungle without the mellowing role and benign intervention of religion. The two must interact rationally and fairly as integral parts of an organic whole without one dominating the other.

Secularism stands for complete religious freedom for all the loyal constituents of the state, as much, in fact more, for the religious minorities than for the religious majority. Where is the Islamic Republic of Pakistan headed for under the rubric of 'Islamic' in the seventh decade of its coming into existence? How could it ever justify the cold-blooded murders by a religious fanatic of a serving provincial governor (Salman Taseer) and federal minister (Shahbaz Bhatti) for allegedly contravening the anti-blasphemy law? Does Prophet Muhammad (PBUH), a blessing for this and the world hereafter need the protection of such a state which is in itself engulfed in a circumstance of a grave, all-embracing crises? The Khatam-e-Nabuwat anti-Qadiani movement in Lahore in 1953, had led to the first martial law. Though confined to the municipal limits of the city, the 1953 martial law was the first stone cast at the glass house of Pakistan's incipient democracy. It was used to upset the politico-constitutional fabric of the state and, as a conspiracy, to dismiss Prime Minister Khawaja Nazimuddin.

Gestating in time, the anti-blasphemy movement developed into law under the military dictator General Mohammad Ziaul Haq. In the garb of 'fundamentalism' Zia brazenly used and abused Islam and absolute devotion and fealty to the Prophet (PBUH) to perpetuate his ersatz caliphate and damage the liberating spirit of Islam.

Although a fledgling yet in the menage of well-established political parties, MQM remains the only party inflexibly opposed to the exploitation of religion for the attainment of political ends. The party's unswerving stand on the issue might have been a literal as well as a true translation of the Quaid's dictum that religion is a matter of the personal faith of the individual.

The emergence of MQM has been a benchmark in Pakistan's party politics torn between dynastic-feudal moorings and pseudo-ideological-theocentric trappings. MQM came with an earthly agenda to project the case of the migrants from India, the Mohajirs, in the wake of massive communal carnage following Partition.

In the first four years, i.e., between 1947–1951, the Mohajir leadership under Prime Minister Liaquat Ali Khan and bureaucrats who had served in the Indian Civil Service (ICS) occupied senior ranks at the Centre. Overwhelmingly Mohajirs, they served the country and the government with absolute devotion to duty and dedication to the country. Liaquat's assassination in October 1951 left the Mohajirs without any political cover. The unceremonious and unlawful dismissal of Prime Minister Khawaja Nazimuddin in April 1953 was yet another blow to the politico-constitutional-demographic unity of the country. Bengalis and Mohajirs found themselves in the same situation; virtually as aliens.

The Ayub Khan period (1958–1969) had been one of deep contempt both for the Mohajirs and the Bengalis. Ayub dismissed one with an unkindly impulsive wave of the hand and the other with some unwelcome remark. Mohajirs, by and large, might have been a pain in the neck whereas the Bengalis a headache—a veritable curse. 'Bengalis', he wrote, in his biography *Friends Not Masters* 'have all the inhibitions of downtrodden races.... They had not known any real freedom or sovereignty....' Such remarks of his were the unkindest affront to all the freedom fighters of Muslim Bengal—Siraj-ud-Daulah, Titu Mian, Shariatullah, his son Dudu Mian and others.

Yahya Khan's disastrous interregnum (1969–1971), had been relatively Mohajir-Bengali friendly. He couldn't care less 'which side of the river one might have been born so long as one delivered the goods'.

Next came Zulfikar Ali Bhutto in 1971 to tread the anti-Mohajir trail. His rule saw the violent eruption of Urdu-Sindhi language riots in October 1972 in Karachi when Bhutto's 'talented cousin' Sardar Mumtaz Ali Bhutto was Governor of Sindh. This situation continued till Bhutto's disastrous end on 5 July 1977.

Pakistan Peoples Party's (PPP) massive rigging in the general elections of March 1977 sparked off a country-wide movement under the banner of Pakistan National Alliance (PNA) that demanded re-elections. PNA was a medley of secular and non-secular (the so-called religious parties) that had come together against PPP for their own opportunistic ends. Failing to estimate the overwhelming popularity of the movement, Bhutto refused to concede to the demand for fresh elections. As a result, law and order broke down and the army had to be called in aid to civil power. Martial law was imposed in Karachi and Lahore. The Army Chief, General Ziaul Haq, who had been waiting in the wings, struck on 5 July 1977. He toppled Bhutto and declared martial law in the country.

Bhutto, along with his senior PPP associates, was placed under 'protective' military custody.

The young students of the University of Karachi, under the leadership of Altaf Hussain, had helped the PNA, especially the Jamaat-e-Islami, all the way through the anti-Bhutto movement. The movement ended traumatically in the dismissal of Bhutto's government by Zia. Not a word of gratitude came forth from the Jamaat for all the hard work that Altaf Hussain and his fellow students had put in to aid the Jamaat. Rank ingratitude on the part of the Jamaat, and also the PNA's thankless revivalist leadership and their Nizam-i-Mustafa programme for the establishment of an Islamic state and society turned Altaf and his group against the Jamaat. The young activist was thoroughly disgusted by the 'devious tactics' used by those who would talk of an Islamic order and claim to be its standard bearers in one breath and behave in a thoroughly unethical manner in the other. Rather than being motivated by the love of Islam, the PNA slogan of 'Islami Nizam or Nizam-e-Mustafa', was mainly a tool to exploit the masses to attain their narrow political ends. As soon as Bhutto, the principal target of their movement was removed from the scene, the movement disintegrated.

Martial Law was welcomed by religio-political parties mainly the Jamaat-e-Islami. Two top leaders of the Jamaat even joined Zia's cabinet as federal ministers. As for the Nizam-e-Mustafa movement, it simply dissolved into thin air. Altaf Hussain and his associates found themselves in the wilderness after the hectic days of the PNA movement.

In the political vacuum following a ban on the mainstream majority Pakistan People's Party, politico-religious parties emerged as the new power-brokers. The Mohajirs of Karachi, especially the student community, were dropped by the wayside after the elections. At the University of Karachi, the student wing of the Jamaat-e-Islami, the Islami Jamiat-i-Tulaba (IJT) emerged as the 'Thunder Squad' and sole organ for 80 per cent of the Mohajir students. Another party also existed which was liberal and progressive. Both these parties were well-entrenched in university politics. Little or no scope was left for a third party. Hence, rather than gate-crashing as a third party, the Altaf group chose to wait.

Students at the University of Karachi, subsequently, split into several ethnic groups—Sindhi, Punjabi, Pakhtun, Baloch, Gilgiti, and so on. Admission to various faculties and access to facilities, particularly living accommodation in hostels, were provided on the basis of provincial connection. The Islami Jamiat-e-Tulaba (IJT) was not an all-Mohajir student group; it had within its ranks a fair share of Punjabis and Pakhtuns as well. The pro-Jamaat Mohajir students in the IJT quit the organization after the elections and, in 1978, launched the All-Pakistan Mohajir Students' Organization (APMSO) under the leadership of Altaf Hussain, a fellow student at the university. MQM's journey as a student body in the form of APMSO in 1978, to a political organ for the Mohajir community as the

Mohajir Quami Movement (MQM) in 1984 and finally culminating in the formation of Muttahida Quami Movement on 26 July 1997. It has been most eventful. Its evolution is no less than a miracle. MQM was formed with two clear objectives: (a) to bring the scattered and practically leaderless Mohajir community on a single platform; (b) to lead them into the political mainstream on a national level.[2]

The Mohajir-Pakhtun confrontation in December 1986, and the ruthless violence and bloodshed perpetrated in the pre-dominantly Mohajir Qasba, Aligarh, and Orangi colonies by the Pakhtun drug mafia, shattered any hope of a Mohajir-non/Mohajir rapport. In the aftermath of the December upheaval, the MQM emerged as a party with a politico-philosophical agenda to serve as a platform from which the Mohajirs could vent all the pent-up frustrations.

The MQM performed well in the non-party Local Bodies polls in 1986 and 1987 gaining municipal control of Karachi and Hyderabad and governing the two cities through its own mayors. In the party-based general elections of 1988, the MQM emerged as the second largest party in Sindh and brokered an alliance with the PPP, the largest single party at both provincial and national levels. The alliance soon collapsed.

The uncanny coincidence of the birth of MQM and General Ziaul Haq's referendum in 1984, confirming his rule for the next five years, is exploited by critics as evidence of its being a protégé of the Army. Nothing could be further from the truth. The same MQM became the sole target of the brutal army Operation Clean-up (also known as Operation Blue Fox) in 1992 on the orders of the Army Chief, General Asif Nawaz Janjua, who made no secret of his desire to split the MQM. He argued that, if there could be more than one Muslim League, why can't there be more than two MQMs? And this was in spite of Altaf Hussain's personal assurances and entreaties to General Janjua of his and MQM's bonafides as a patriotic party and its abiding loyalty to the army and the country. Under the Operation Clean-up of 1992, MQM's offices in Karachi and Hyderabad were raided by police and Rangers. The so-called torture cells were ferreted out in no time and a bogus parallel organization MQM (Haqiqi), was created through party dissidents—Afaq Ahmed, Amir Khan, and Badar Iqbal.

A murder attempt was made on Altaf Hussain's life soon afterwards, while he was admitted in hospital, forcing him to flee the country the same year. That should have been enough to disprove the theory that MQM was the creation of the army. The truth was that the two bodies could not be more at divergence to each other.

In the course of my two extended meetings [not formal interviews] with Altaf Hussain: first, at No. 4 Halegroves Gardens, London, in July 1994; and the second, at the MQM International Secretariat Middlesex, London, in July 1996, we discussed at length almost all the points already covered in this narrative. Oddly enough

I never got the opportunity to meet Altaf Hussain in Karachi.[3]

At the very start of our first meeting I asked Mr Hussain to tell me how to address him whether as a youngster or a party leader. His unhesitant reply was: 'youngster, Sir' thus creating the right setting for our conversation. I found Altaf Hussain a patient listener. He'd expect the same from his interlocutor in turn.

Born in 1953, at the time of our meeting, he stood at the threshold of middle age at 37 still full of youthful energy. He had nothing of the physical charisma of a Jinnah, or of a Bhutto, or of a Nehru but a sort of an aura of authority. Dressed in typical Nehru-cut jacket, long *kurta* and white, narrow-bottomed Aligarh-style pajama he looked as simple as a middle class Karachiite. He smoked moderately.

Taking advantage as an elder (*buzurg*) I addressed him as '*Mian*', a rare deviation from the stock 'Altaf Bhai'. It was hard for me to grasp the fact that I was sitting in front of a man whose voice would be heard by multitudes —all Mohajirs—in hushed silence and whose every word would be considered as a decree by his followers.

Altaf waited for me to begin the conversation. I expressed some of my own misgivings about the very foundation of MQM as an exclusive body accounting for a minuscule minority in a country dominated by power-ful ethnic groups—each with its own home base.

After the separation of East Pakistan, the ethnic divide had become so wide that it left little space for a Baloch,

Pakhtun, or a Punjabi to live as a fellow citizen outside of
his/her own provincial milieu. As for Mohajirs, they were
everywhere and yet nowhere: '*Yak su randah digar su
durmandha*' (driven out from one side and worn-out on
the other). They carried the stigma of 'Mohajir' in spite of
their absolute commitment and loyalty to Pakistan.

My other question to him was about the emergence
of MQM as a powerful Mohajir party doing more harm
than good to them as a community. I cited the launching
of the army's Operation Clean-up against the MQM as
evidence of the rising anti-Mohajir sentiment in the
country, more particularly, in the predominant Mohajir
strongholds: Karachi, Hyderabad, Sukkur, Nawabshah
and other such areas of Sindh. It was a sort of a rambling
discourse on my part to highlight the futility of any effort
to have Mohajirs recognized as a distinctive entity with
their own language, dress, and culture in their own
province. Altaf Hussain (I would use '*Mian*' only while
addressing him directly) heard me out with commend-
able patience looking straight into my eyes.

'Would you agree on whether the emergence of MQM
had made more enemies than friends by choosing to go
alone?' The opening ambit of Altaf Hussain's response to
my question was the sad tale of the excesses committed
against the Urdu-speaking Mohajirs particularly by the
army. He was especially bitter against General Asif Nawaz
Janjua. He stressed that the amount of damage General
Asif Nawaz alone did to the MQM exceeded any other
done to the party and the community. Janjua not only

hated the MQM but also despised the entire Mohajir community. He [Altaf Hussain] went all the way to convince the General of his and MQM's loyalty and love for the country. But all in vain. General Nawaz spared no efforts to break up the party. He pitted Afaq Ahmed, Amir Khan, Badar Iqbal and others against Altaf as alternate Mohajir leaders.

After General Nawaz's sudden death in January 1993, General Abdul Waheed Kakar (1993–1996) a 'Benazir loyalist' would show much the same antipathy to the MQM. After him, General Jehangir Karamat (1996–1998) though relatively less aggressive, displayed more or less the same unsympathetic attitude towards the party. Altaf's concluding remark to me was: 'Siddiqi Sahib, nature intervenes when human effort either fails or is not made at the right time to stem the rot.' Have events come full circle to confront us with the wages of our sins of omission and commission? The question is not for an individual or two but for the whole community to answer.[4]

Ayesha Jalal writes that the Mohajir dilemma in Pakistan, remains as complex as before. To their inherent sense of *otherness* has been added what Ayesha Jalal calls *else* (*ness*), a state of mind in the context of their changed relationships with the Indian Muslims and Bangladeshis, once their fellow citizens and kinsmen, now strangers and foreigners with little in common expect haunting memories of a shared past.

The lot of the Pakistani Biharis remains the most pathetic and lamentable. They stand completely denationalized, ostracized, and disowned, rotting in the squalor of their Bangladeshi camps as 'muhasareen'—a people under siege. The dramatic shifts in nationality from Indian to Pakistani, from Pakistani to Bangladeshi-turned-Bihari without a country have been mind-boggling. . . .[5]

Brigadier (R) Abdul Rahman Siddiqi
Executive Director
Regional Institute for Peace and Security
Pakistan

Notes

1. I have borrowed liberally and quoted selectively from my two seminal works on the subject—*Mohajir* (Urdu), (Azad Publishers, Lahore), 1997 and *Partition and the Making of the Mohajir Mindset* (Oxford University Press, Karachi), 2008.
2. For a detailed survey of the evolution of MQM from Mohajir to Muttahida see the author's *Mohajir* (Urdu), Azad Publisher's Lahore, 1997.
3. See *Mohajir*, pp. 265–95.
4. For an extended coverage of my meeting with Altaf Sahib, see *Mohajir*, pp. 265–95.
5. Ayesha Jalal, *Self and Sovereignty: Individual and Community in South Asian Islam since 1850* (New York/London: Routledge), 2001.

An Important Clarification

The book *Safar-e-Zindagi* was compiled in 1988. It is based on the events of Mr Altaf Hussain's life up to the year 1988. In 1988, the Mohajir Quami Movement sought to ensure the rights of oppressed Mohajirs, hence readers are requested to regard this book in the context of being up to 1988.

Almost ten years later, on 26 July 1997, the Mohajir Quami Movement became the Muttahida Quami Movement, and the field of this struggle was expanded to a nationwide level. The goal of the movement is to secure the rights of all the deprived and oppressed people of Pakistan; to rescue them from tyranny and exploitation, as well as to wipe out the obsolete feudal system prevailing in the country. This book will give readers a good idea of how harsh and trying the state of affairs was, the events that occurred and the trials which Mr Altaf Hussain, the leader of the Muttahida Quami Movement, had to pass through in the early years of his struggle, before he arrived at his present eminence.

We hope, in fact we are convinced, that this book will inspire new courage and new determination in every individual who wishes to bring about a revolution in society and thus help and encourage them in their dream.

DR IMRAN FAROOQ
Convener, Muttahida Quami Movement

Acronyms and Abbreviations

ANP	Awami National Party
APMSO	All-Pakistan Mohajir Students' Organization
CIA	Central Intelligence Agency
CSP	Civil Service of Pakistan
CSS	Central Superior Services
DC	Deputy Commissioner
DSP	Deputy Superintendent of Police
FIR	First Information Report
IBA	Institute of Business Administration
KESC	Karachi Electric Supply Corporation
MPA	Member of Provincial Assembly
MQM	Mohajir Quami Movement
	(now Muttahida Quami Movement)
NDP	National Democratic Party
NOC	No Objection Certificate
NWFP	North-West Frontier Province
PIA	Pakistan International Airlines
PNA	Pakistan National Alliance
PPP	Pakistan People's Party
PRC	Permanent Residence Certificate
PSA	Punjab Students' Alliance
SDM	Sub-Divisional Magistrate
SHO	Station House Officer
SP	Superintendent of Police
SSP	Senior Superintendent of Police
US	United States
WAPDA	Water and Power Development Authority

Part I

The Struggle and Birth of the MQM

1

Early Perceptions and the National Cadet Service

During my childhood in the early sixties, we lived in a small quarter on Jehangir Road where government employees were housed. I remember one incident vividly of those days. In 1964, when Ayub Khan 'defeated' Quaid-i-Azam Mohammad Ali Jinnah's sister, Miss Fatima Jinnah, in the presidential elections, Ayub Khan's son, Gohar Ayub decided to 'celebrate' his father's victory in Karachi. That day is etched in my memory. I was bringing my mother back from my uncle's house to ours on Jehangir Road. When our rickshaw approached Filmistan Cinema, between Lasbella and Teenhatti, we found that the traffic had stopped and there was panic and commotion all around us. The rickshaw driver informed us nervously that the Pakhtuns were on the rampage and told us to get out of the vehicle. I was quite confused but, nevertheless, took my mother's hand and we got off the rickshaw. We saw people carrying guns, rods, and iron bars. We were very scared. In front of us were government quarters. I knocked at the doors of several houses but the occupants were too scared to let us in. Finally, we found shelter in one of them. I kept asking people the cause of the commotion but the only answer I got was that the Pakhtuns had attacked the Mohajirs. What I wanted to know was what had the Mohajirs done to incur such wrath, I was told that the Mohajirs were being punished because they had supported Fatima Jinnah against Ayub Khan in the elections.

The treatment meted out to unarmed citizens of Karachi on that occasion is a shameful chapter of our national history. This episode left a deep impression on my mind. That was the first time I realized that there was a parochial bias in our environment; that there was an element that discriminated people on ethnic lines. There was constant talk of who was a Sindhi, Punjabi, or Pakhtun. Nobody ever called themselves Pakistani.

Many of our neighbours in the government quarters came from different parts of Pakistan and spoke different languages of the country. They included Bengalis who, too, were employees of the Pakistan government in those days. I was friendly with their children, as well as the children of neighbours belonging to other parts of Pakistan, and would often visit them. One evening I was visiting a Bengali friend of mine. Many of his relatives were also present in his house and they were all having a passionate discussion. I could not follow everything they were saying but the gist of it was that they wanted to break free from Pakistan and make a separate Bengali state.

I asked those people, 'Why do you want to do that? After all, we made a lot of sacrifices to get Pakistan.' They told me their reasons but I was too young to grasp their meaning fully. Later, I told my Bengali friend, 'Do explain to your relatives that we worked very hard to get Pakistan and made many sacrifices. They should not think of breaking away from it.' The fact is that I loved Pakistan as a child and, to this day, my love is undiminished and remains as deep as it ever was. The blood of our forebears runs in the foundations of this country; a fact that nobody can deny, but I am sorry to say that the sacrifices made for achieving Pakistan have never been expressed clearly. Neither the electronic nor the print media have ever pointed out the sacrifices made by Muslims of the minority provinces of British India. The fact that the people of these areas courted death for themselves and their children in order to gain Pakistan has never been mentioned, nor is their contribution in this regard remembered, commemorated, or properly recorded so that it may be passed down from one generation to the next.

To go back to my Bengali friend, I was then in sixth or seventh grade at school and was hardly in a position to convince him or his family to change their views. Finally, in 1971, the inevitable happened and East Pakistan became Bangladesh.

My family loved Pakistan with fervour and passion and, from a very tender age, they had inculcated a deep sense of patriotism within me. I remember clearly my feelings in 1965 when Pakistan and India went to war. I must have been about 11 years old then and my emotional involvement in the war was tremendous. I used to listen attentively to the news on the radio. It was my earnest desire to somehow join the army and go to the battlefront though, of course, I was too young at that time for my wish to be realized.

I remember that, during that war, bomb shelters had been dug in various parts of the city. Our neighbourhood, too, had bomb shelters. To assuage our desire to fight in the war, I and other children of the area used to play games in which we would form a Pakistan army and an Indian army. We would imagine the bomb shelter was our bunker and we would go into it and the 'Indian army' would attack the 'Pakistan army'. The latter, of which I was inevitably a part, would then defend itself strongly. By playing those games, all of us children, who dreamt of joining the army and defending our borders when we grew up, were reassuring ourselves that indeed, some day, our wish would come true.

Before the 1965 war, I wanted to be a doctor when I grew up. But the war brought about a change in my thinking and I decided to join the army in order to defend my country. I think it was in 1970 when I was a student of Inter Science at City College in Karachi, that Yahya Khan's government started a mandatory military service scheme known as the National Cadet Service Scheme. Under this scheme, every young man who had completed Matriculation was obliged to put in a year's military service. Therefore, all colleges began the process of selecting candidates for the first year's course.

I desperately wanted to be selected but knew that I had no sources of recommendation since my family lacked influence. A selection team from the army came to our college and all candidates took an admission test, including myself. When the results came out and I heard that I had qualified for the National Cadet Service my joy knew no bounds. I took some money from my parents and bought sweets which I distributed among my friends in the neighbourhood. After the selection we were sent for training.

The initial training session was at the Karachi Cantonment but, after a few days, we were taken to the Hyderabad Cantonment. While we were still training there, war broke out in East Pakistan. News of it made me really restless and I yearned to go to the battlefield and fight for my country. During the training period we used to have physical training in the evenings. One day, after the physical training session, I went to change into my regular clothes. As I was picking up my clothes from my upper bunk bed, I heard loud cries of 'Nara-e-Takbir Allah-o-Akbar' from outside. I knew immediately that the war had begun on the Western Front that is West Pakistan. I ran outside without putting on my kameez. A lot of young trainees were assembled there and they informed me that indeed fighting had begun in the Western Wing. Hearing this piece of news, I was immeasurably delighted to think that now we would definitely be sent to the front. This was the good news the other cadets and I had been longing to hear. Every day we used to plead with our instructors and the army officers present to forward our request to be sent to the front, to the right quarters.

Finally, one night at about 1 a.m., we were ordered to pack our belongings. In accordance with military code, we desisted from trying to find out our destination but we realized that we were being sent to some battlefront. We were put on a train in Hyderabad. The train made frequent stops *en route* to Karachi in order to avoid aerial bombing that was being carried out by enemy aircrafts continuously throughout the night. Consequently, it took us about fifteen hours to get from Hyderabad to Karachi. At Karachi Cantonment we were transferred to trucks which took us to a transit camp located nearby. It was only when we arrived there that we got to know that we were being sent to East Pakistan because the weapons we had been trained to use were those for close combat.

Two of our detachments were taken to Keamari, where they were to board a ship for East Pakistan but they returned after two days because of the Indian blockade of East Pakistan. This state of affairs came as a shock to me because I had been under the illusion that my dreams were about to be realized. Karachi was being bombed frequently and oil tankers that were berthed in Keamari had also been targeted; a situation which served to make us even more livid. Enemy bombers flew low over the sea, which was why our radars did not pick them up, and thus they were able to enter the airspace of Karachi.

During this period, the decision was taken to convert the National Cadet Service Scheme into the 57 Baloch Regiment. Accordingly, we were given the name of 57 Baloch Regiment, loaded into trucks, and sent to Sonmiani, a port on the Makran coast near the Balochistan Sector, because it was from there that the enemy planes flew into Pakistan's airspace. On the way to Sonmiani we felt elated once again because we thought that now, at last, we will fight in the war, kill our enemies and, if need be, happily give up our own lives for our country.

After our arrival in Sonmiani, we set up camp and started preparations for building our defence. We dug trenches and occupied them but, unfortunately, the war ended a few days later. However, our Commander decided that 57 Baloch Regiment, which consisted entirely of cadets whose training had been confined to cantonments and who had not been given any border training, would receive this part of their training in Sonmiani.

Thereafter we became happily engaged in completing our border training in Sonmiani. However, what is noteworthy about this period is that I experienced a number of occurrences which were at first incomprehensible to me but, once I understood them, I found them extremely painful.

We were divided into two teams during border training. In night training we were taught how to attack the enemy and how to defend ourselves when the enemy attacked, as well as how to go into the forests and attack the enemy in its trenches.

We noticed that every day we were selected for the team that had to trudge long distances through hills and forests to arrive at the designated trenches that we were supposed to attack. At first we were happy about this because we thought that we were being given tougher training; that those who were made to work harder were expected to perform better. However, later we learned that the treatment we were being meted out was because of a very different line of thought: The sergeant in charge of us used to have those he favoured sit in the ditches near the camp and would send the rest of us off on the double along lengthy and difficult routes. Although, even when we came to this realization, we did not consider it a great drawback for ourselves because we thought that the hard work involved would toughen us and make us better soldiers in the long run.

During the training, one exercise was that one team would hide in the ditches and the other would demonstrate its ability to attack it from a secret position. A line was drawn near the ditch. If the attacking team crossed it and cried 'Charge!', it won; but if the team hidden in the ditch cried 'Halt!' before the attackers crossed the line, that was declared the winning team. One day, we were in the attacking team. We managed to approach the ditch crawling and without being detected and I shouted 'Charge!' loudly as we crossed the line. But as soon as I said 'Charge', the team hidden in the ditch shouted 'Halt!' Our sergeant was present on that occasion and he turned on me and reprimanded me, 'Ho! What are you blathering about?'

'Sir, I said "Charge" first,' I told him.

'Who said you were first?' he retorted. And then he added something that at first I didn't understand: 'Who selected you in the army? You people from Karachi; living in big cities; drinking tea; wearing teddy trousers! How can you fight a war?' The man then abused not only me but also everybody who came from cities.

I was deeply hurt and very angry. I said to him, 'Sir, I had so looked forward to joining the army but now you say how can anybody from Karachi fight a war!'

Hearing the man's remarks I lost the enthusiasm that had filled me since childhood. I had joined the army with great fervour, expectations, and hope; with intense feelings of passion and my only aim was to die for my country! The sergeant's words had crushed my dreams.

I reported the incident to the *subedar* major reminding him that superior army officers who came to lecture us used to say in all their speeches that the army was an institution where the high and the low received the same treatment. I told him what the sergeant had said to me and added that, whereas I had come with great expectations, this was how I was being treated.

The sergeant was summoned as a result of my complaint. I was happily expecting that justice would be meted out and was waiting impatiently for the verdict. However, instead of 'justice', I was punished for breach of discipline. I was sentenced to do '*pitthu* parade' for a week.

As a result of this incident, I began to notice a lot of other things. Even though my feelings were badly hurt, I had not given up hope. I did not allow my mind to harbour negative thoughts nor did I adopt a negative attitude. I tried to pacify my wounded sensibilities by telling myself that the sergeant's views were the views of one individual only, and that if I encountered such views from anyone I would try my best to correct them.

During the period of my training, I tried with all sincerity to execute all exercises and assignments responsibly in order to acquire the capability of using this training for the defence of my country, if ever such services were required. This was my attitude despite the fact that I was aware that some people were being given discriminatory treatment. For example, the place where our ration and other items of use were stored was at some distance from the camp and we were always ordered to lug firewood and other stuff from there all the way to our camp. Moreover, the night pass that we needed to go home for the weekend was also issued on a discriminatory basis.

I tried to persuade other Mohajir boys who were with me in the programme that we needed to speak about this matter to our officers but, though at first they agreed with me, fear of the consequences made them change their mind.

2

Education

Admission into the B.Sc. Course

After we had completed our year's training, we were taken to Karachi Cantonment where we were given our release orders. It was during this period of training that I realized for the first time that, in our country, many people thought in terms of parochial differences. I was very disturbed by this as never before had I thought along such lines or heard such biased attitudes voiced. What I believed in and desired was for Pakistani people to be united.

In 1972, after completing my military training, I took admission in the B.Sc. (pre-medical) course offered by Islamia Science College. While I completed the course there and earned my B.Sc. degree, I also worked towards eradicating biases from the minds of people around me, urging them that they should forget all 'isms' and call themselves 'Pakistanis' and nothing else.

Admission into B. Pharmacy

After completing my B.Sc. from Islamia College, I applied to the University of Karachi for admission to the

B. Pharmacy course. Unfortunately by the time the results of our final exams came out, admissions to B. Pharmacy had closed. Students who were affected by this lacuna and could not get admission to B. Pharmacy spoke to the Vice Chancellor of the university and other responsible officials informing them that our results were announced late, which was no fault of ours, and, if we were not admitted, we would waste a whole year without having done anything to deserve this. But we were still refused admission. Consequently, we formed a 'B.Sc. Action Committee', and held several peaceful protests. This action had become necessary because the matter affected the future of almost 200 students. We put up banners, demonstrated with placards and pressed our demand that we be admitted into the B. Pharmacy course. We met the teachers of the course, the Academic Council and members of the University's Syndicate, and explained our problem to them. We tried to make them realize that, to deprive us of admission to the course because our results were announced late, was patently unjust especially since it was the University of Karachi that ran the B. Pharmacy course and that it was the university that had announced our results late. For their own mistake they had closed their doors on us.

We continued our protest and, because there seemed to be very little chance of success, most of our companions deserted us. Finally, only forty students remained who came to the university everyday and took active part in the protest.

When discussions and peaceful protests failed to produce positive results, our Action Committee decided to go on hunger strike. As the chairman of this committee, I took the first step. We continued the fight doggedly for nine months. When the university administration saw our persistence, they tried to break up our movement by announcing that they would grant admission to some of the protesting students. I was extremely distressed to see that the boys who were granted admission in this way immediately accepted and abandoned the movement. On the other hand, the university administration had previously proposed to me several times that they would give me admission if I disbanded the Action Committee. They had even gone to the extent of offering to me to recommend two of my friends whom they would accommodate as well. Each time my response had been, 'I have not been running this movement for nine months to get admission only for myself and two of my friends. Admission must be given to all the members of the movement or else nobody from amongst us would accept it.'

After those of our companions who had accepted the offer left us, I told the remaining members to have courage and not to lose heart.

Subsequently, I began to meet members of the Academic Council and the Syndicate individually and explained to them that the administration had offered admission to some students simply to sabotage our movement. I am very grateful to those members for their integrity and fair-mindedness which resulted in the cancellation of those admissions by the administration. Finally, our movement was successful and all of us were granted admission into B. Pharmacy.

3

The Role of the Students' Unions

Besides Mohajir students, our Action Committee had included Punjabi and Pakhtun students and I made sure that all of them were admitted at the same time as we. This was because I disliked prejudice and wanted to put an end to it.

Here I would like to mention something that made a deep impression on me. When I first went to the University of Karachi, I saw banners there which proclaimed: 'Pakhtun Students' Federation', 'Jiye Sindh Students' Federation', 'Punjabi Students' Association', 'Baloch Students' Organization', 'Kashmiri Students' Federation', 'Gilgit Students' Federation', 'Tribal Students' Federation', etc. I was astonished to see these banners and slogans and wondered, 'what was the need for the formation of these organizations?' However, to date, my question has not been answered.

Those banners and slogans forced me to think about my identity and those of my people since we are not Baloch, Punjabis, Sindhis, Kashmiris, Gilgitis or tribals. We are, of course, Pakistanis but the rest of the people seemed to base their identity on ethnicity. The next question that came to my mind was, 'why and for what purpose were these organizations formed?' The answer to this question, I learned, was the following:

There were three important and influential student organizations. One was the Islami Jamiat-e-Tulaba; the second was the Progressive Students' Organization; and the third was Pakistan Liberal Students' Organization. When elections came around, these three organizations made deals with those that were based on ethnicity and parochialism and accommodated one or the other of their candidates on their own panels in order to get the votes from that ethnic group.

I found this situation astounding. The Progressives claimed to be progressive but, at election time, they invariably made deals with ethnic organizations like the 'Pakhtun Students' Federation', the 'Jiye Sindh Students' Federation' or 'Tribal Students' etc. Similarly, the Islami Jamiat-e-Tulaba always allied itself with the Punjabi Students' Association. This meant that, when there were elections in the University of Karachi, the student organizations that, at other times, proclaimed egalitarian slogans of universality, fairness, etc., allied themselves with ethnic organizations simply to gain votes and thus, in effect, promoted parochialism, prejudice and disunity. I felt that, at least, the Progressives, Liberals, and Islami Jamiat-e-Tulaba should not have done this since the first two claimed to be progressive and the Jamiat talked of the brotherhood of Islam. Regarding the Jamiat, since it allied itself with the Punjab Students' Alliance (PSA), the result was that the PSA would dominate it and selected candidates would be given seats. What was amazing was that most of Jamiat's members were Mohajirs. However, if you look at the list of their office-bearers, a different picture emerges.

With this state of affairs prevailing, students who comprised the majority found it harder to gain admission into the university or, if they were admitted, they were not allotted rooms in the students' hostel. As for the regional organizations, they held protests outside the Vice Chancellor's office whenever they liked and, by forming pressure groups, they could coerce them into admitting their students while hundreds of Karachi students had nowhere to go. So I wondered whether the Karachi students had any representatives of their own to voice their concerns. What I would have liked to have seen was that, instead of granting admission to the University of Karachi on the basis of ethnicity or parochialism, students were selected purely on the basis of merit. Since the university is situated in Karachi, it is only fair that the students who come from Karachi have the first right to admissions here just as students of other cities should have the first right to admissions to the universities in their respective cities. At the University of Karachi, however, there were quotas for different groups coming from other provinces. It was hard to understand this difference between Karachi and other cities. As for the students' hostels, they were completely under the control of the regional organizations.

Boys from Karachi rarely got a room in a hostel or, if they did manage to get one, it was because of the patronage of one of the three aforementioned powerful organizations. Since many students in Karachi live in houses that are very small or consist of a single room, they are deprived of a study-friendly environment. Thus, it was my suggestion that they should be accommodated in hostels. But the response that I received was that there were no rooms available for them. Despite all this, my endeavour was that people should stop talking of ethnicity and parochialism and start thinking as one nation—as being simply Pakistanis.

4

The Idea of a Fifth Nationality

I recalled the dreadful day the Pakhtuns attacked the Mohajirs in 1964 and also the attitude I encountered among my officers during my stint with the National Cadet Service Scheme. About this time we frequently heard of situations where someone's father or uncle had been forced to retire, that someone was unable to find a job because he did not have recourse to any sort of recommendation, or because he was not a 'son of the soil'. Though only a student in those days, I was acutely conscious that people who ought to be calling themselves Pakistani were not doing so. As for 'sons of the soil', I discovered that this term was used for those who lived in areas which constituted Pakistan before Partition.

It seemed that it was considered that those who had migrated to Pakistan from India did not belong to this category even though my contemporaries and I had been born and bred in Karachi and had received primary to higher education in Karachi. These matters naturally generated a lot of questions in my mind but, when I set about trying to find answers, no answer was forthcoming.

In Ayub Khan's days, Mohajir civil servants and other government employees were sacked and the same thing happened under Yahya Khan and Zulfikar Ali Bhutto. Yet, despite all this, Mohajirs retained an unshakeable faith in the unity of Pakistan and its people. They had given their blood for this country; they had sacrificed everything for it. They had left behind (in India) their ancestors' graves, the streets where they had played and spent their childhood, and had given up the shrines of their saints. During Partition, more than two million Muslims from the Muslim-minority provinces of India were slain. It was only then that Pakistan came into being. It is because of the heavy price Mohajirs have paid that they are fundamentally very emotional about Pakistan and Islam and, for these two ideals, they were ready to make the highest sacrifice.

It was incomprehensible why every head of government targeted the Mohajirs even though they were the only people who thought along nationalistic lines and did not identify themselves with any ethnic group. On the other hand I have seen, on many occasions that leaders tend to identify with their own ethnic community. Under Bhutto, clashes over language were engineered and the victims were the Mohajirs who suffered atrocities in their own city. However, these developments did not go unnoticed by the Mohajirs which was perhaps the reason why, in the general elections during Bhutto's rule, they supported the Pakistan National Alliance (PNA).

5

My Role in the Nizam-e-Mustafa Movement

In 1977, when the Pakistan People's Party government announced their decision to hold elections, the Opposition formed the Quami Ittehad (Pakistan National Alliance) in which they could unite in order to confront the Pakistan People's Party. The Mohajirs decided to support the national alliance. The language clashes were fresh in their minds, they were suffering from discrimination in their search for jobs, and Mohajir students were treated unfairly in educational institutions. Thus, they were compelled towards joining the PNA.

After the elections, the results were rejected on charges of rigging and the Nizam-e-Mustafa (Islamic system of governance) Movement was launched. The sacrifices Mohajirs made for this movement were not based on enmity for Bhutto or the Pakistan People's Party; they were based solely on their aspirations and their slogan that had led to the creation of Pakistan. This slogan was, 'We are not Baloch, Sindhi, Punjabi or Pakhtun. We are only Pakistanis and Muslims.' The general belief was that, once Nizam-e-Mustafa was established in Pakistan, prejudice, injustice, and oppression would cease.

I remember well that the leaders of the PNA would openly tell Mohajirs that injustice had been done to them and the Pakistan People's Party had persecuted them. They would further say that, when the PNA came to power, it would put an end to the oppression of Mohajirs and abolish the quota system. I used to believe what they said because, in those days, my understanding of their politics did not extend deep enough for me to be aware of the secret objectives which controlled their actions. We believed that this was a movement that would bring in the true Nizam-e-Mustafa and the establishment of this order would be beneficial for the country. We did not realize at the time that it was simply a rallying slogan to bring all the parties together. Perhaps this was the first time in the history of the country that all the political parties and leaders, including Wali Khan, were participating in one movement—the PNA. G.M. Syed, too, had announced his unconditional support for it. This meant that everybody wanted change. I don't want to go into the details of who, and to what degree, was sincere in raising the slogan but, as far as the Mohajirs were concerned, they supported the PNA purely for the sake of Islam and Pakistan. Nobody in the entire country gave the kind of sacrifices that the Mohajirs in Sindh gave until the movement lasted.

I was a student in those days and, because I had been a victim of bigotry and prejudice myself, I keenly desired a change in society; so I was drawn towards the movement. I participated in the PNA as a humble worker and went wherever a meeting was held. I wanted that our aim should be only Pakistan and Islam, and having been taken in by the PNA slogans which proclaimed that they would change the whole system and put an end to injustice and oppression, I worked wholeheartedly for them. I asked my mother, '*Ammi*, the leaders of Quami Ittehad talk of Pakistan and Islam; so please give me permission to work for them. I might even lose my life in serving this cause but do not worry on that account.'

6

My Involvement with the Pakistan National Alliance (PNA)

Indeed I was impressed by the PNA's slogan and gave them preference above other groups because the movement included Punjabis, Baloch, Pakhtuns and Mohajirs all working for one ideal. Under this movement, Students' Action Committees were formed in different areas. Seeing the sincerity of my service, I was made Chairman of the Action Committee from Federal B Area. We were a very active group and would hold meetings in mosques as well as demonstrations.

One day we were told suddenly that there was to be a meeting in a local mosque after *Isha* prayers (the night-time daily prayers). It was suggested in that meeting that, since a lot of people had joined the Committee, an election should be held to choose the office bearers. I found it strange that this issue had been raised. Soon I discovered that the Jamaat-e-Islami had raised it. I was not a member of the Jamaat and had not been informed about this action in advance. Had I known about it, I would have prepared myself for the elections.

Actually the meeting had been pre-planned in order to gain certain objectives and most of the people present were followers of the Jamaat. The result was that my opponent, who was from the Islami Jamiat-e-Tulaba (the students' wing of the Jamaat), received thirty-one votes while I got twenty-seven. Had I known about the election earlier, I could have brought many more of my supporters and there would have been no question of my losing. Apparently this was a deliberate move to oust me from the position of Chairman of the Committee. When the people of the area heard the news, they were extremely upset because my efforts and achievements in the field were well known. Seeing the mood of the workers the party had to rethink their action and, finally, they made me General Secretary of the Students' Action Committee. However, I would like to say that these manipulations neither decreased my dedication nor caused me to lessen my efforts for the movement. I do not believe that one should work only for an office. If one is striving for an ideal, such things are meaningless. I had been working hard as an ordinary party worker even before the Students' Action Committee was formed. However, I was sorry to observe the devious tactics employed by people who talked of an Islamic order and claimed to be its standard-bearers.

In the meetings held in those days, the audience would invariably insist that I give a speech. Nobody wrote my speeches. I used to speak extempore and the people appreciated the simplicity and passion in my words. After the speech, people would come up and embrace me and shake hands with me. I remember that once at a meeting of the PNA in block 10 or 12 of Federal B Area, as I was descending the stage after giving a speech, a little boy came to me with his autograph book and a pen. It was the first time that anybody had asked me for an autograph and my mind went completely blank. What on earth was I supposed to write? It was only when the child prodded me with, 'Altaf Bhai, won't you give me your autograph?' that I collected myself and nervously wrote my signature in the child's book.

In those days I noticed that anything I said in meetings during a speech was contradicted by the PNA speaker who came after me. I felt that, since we were supposed to be on the same platform and struggling for the same cause, such contradictions could create a negative impression on the audience. Indeed, they would think there was dissension among us.

Finally, when this happened repeatedly, I complained to the PNA's *Nazim* of Federal B Area and informed him that I would not be delivering any speeches in the future, but I was prepared to do any other kind of work assigned to me such as distributing pamphlets or sticking posters. I told him that we could not afford to divide the audience and disillusion them. The *Nazim* took me with him to the mosque. He told me that he would admonish those who had contradicted me. Nevertheless, I stood my ground and refused to give any more speeches.

In those days the PNA used to hold several meetings in the same town or city on the same day and, since the central leadership attended each of those meetings, they could not naturally, be punctual at every venue. Thus the crowd often had to wait for some time before the key leaders arrived. Meanwhile, in the interim period, the organizers felt the need for someone who could attract a crowd and keep their interest from flagging to give a speech. They once came running to my house and said, 'Altaf, forget everything else and just come to the meeting.' Therefore, once again, I started giving speeches for the sake of the PNA. Often I had to speak for an hour or even longer until the leaders arrived at the meeting.

During the days of the PNA, I noticed that, although there were individuals from all four provinces in its leadership, among the public the movement was concentrated mainly in Karachi, Hyderabad, and some other cities of Sindh. I thought deeply about this aspect but failed to find an answer. I remember well that there had been a 'Long March' in Rawalpindi. However, even for that people went from Karachi and Hyderabad to participate in it. Similarly, in the demonstration that was held outside the Assembly in Lahore, a large number of the demonstrators had come from Karachi and Hyderabad. On the other hand, many newspapers and magazines tried to play down the struggle and sacrifices of the people of Karachi and Hyderabad. I found this attitude most disturbing.

During the PNA movement, the frequency of shootings that occurred on the people of Karachi is unmatched by anything that happened in the rest of the country. Liaquatabad was often subjected to arbitrary bursts of firing. Hyderabad, Mirpurkhas, and other towns of Sindh with large Mohajir populations were similarly treated.

In Lahore, however, the government changed after a single incident of firing. The same government had ordered heavy firing in Sindh, bombed Balochistan, and subjected NWFP (now Khyber Pakhtunkhwa) to violence, with no such repercussions.

Anyhow, as soon as martial law was announced, most political and religio-political parties welcomed it.

7

The Moving Spirit of
the Mohajir Movement

After my association with the PNA, my impressions about many things began to change very fast. I realized that Mohajirs were considered third class citizens and no respect was shown for their lives and possessions. In educational institutions, government and semi-government institutions, in matters of employment or admissions they were considered dispensable. Even in the PNA, sacrifices were accepted from Mohajirs but nobody compensated them for their losses nor rewarded them for their efforts; nor did anybody want to acknowledge their prominent role in the movement. I came to the conclusion that Mohajirs would continue to die, lose all they possessed, and just be exploited. I was convinced that this state of affairs would not change until they had an organization of their own which could speak on their behalf. Therefore, I began to work towards bringing the Mohajirs, at least at the student level, onto one platform. I wished that there existed an organization at the public level, too, which could raise a voice against the injustices meted out to them and provide succour to the victims. But, unfortunately, there was no such organization. Now and then, if from some sector a voice was raised for the Mohajirs, it became quiet or was silenced after a few days. When I probed deeper into this, I found that usually such statements emanated from the shelter of some rich household or the other and, therefore, never amounted to being more than just 'drawing room politics'. Consequently, in 1977, I began to work on a scheme to establish such an organization for the Mohajirs starting at the student level.

When martial law was proclaimed, the political and religio-political parties welcomed it. I was not surprised at this reaction but was amazed at the response of the religio-political parties. Invaluable sacrifices had been made by the people in expectation that the Islamic system or Nizam-e-Mustafa would be established when the PNA came into power. The people had not made sacrifices in order to bring in martial law. But, in the light of what transpired, it became clear that the goal of the movement had been directed solely at removing Bhutto from power and was fuelled by hatred of Bhutto and the Pakistan People's Party. The slogan of *Islami Nizam* was merely a tool used to mobilize the people and instigate them to make sacrifices. The biggest proof of this is that, not only did these parties welcome martial law but also many religio-political and political parties even accepted ministerial positions in the martial law government. And, though when seeking the support of the Mohajirs during the movement they had categorically affirmed that the quota system was wrong and would be abolished, these same gentlemen when appointed ministers, not only did nothing to get rid of the quota system but also even maintained that it was necessary!

The people who accuse the MQM today of dealing in the politics of violence would do well to take a look at their own past. What do these claimants to peace and our political and religio-political leaders have to say about the hundreds of lives and property worth millions of rupees lost during the PNA movement? Would they like to tell us what purpose was served, what gains were made for the good of the people by the slogan and the movement which they espoused? Did they establish the Nizam-e-Mustafa?

8

Who was Responsible for the Language Clashes in Sindh?

The language clashes in Sindh were the result of a conspiracy whose purpose was to fan conflict between the Sindhis and the Mohajirs while the exploiting class retained their positions in the government. This same class of exploiters had previously instigated clashes between the Pakhtuns and the Mohajirs and then between the Sindhis and the Mohajirs. Thus, this exploiting class has always aspired to sow the seeds of hatred between the Sindhis and Mohajirs so that these two groups who inhabit the same land, share the crops that grow on that land, share the water that flows in that river, and, after death, are buried on the same land, who spend their earnings on that land and do not transfer them elsewhere will remain at loggerheads with each other. So this policy, too, was a conspiracy.

The language clashes were responsible for creating enmity between the Sindhis and the Mohajirs. A gulf of hostility was created which did a great deal of damage.

The Sindhis retained feelings of Sindhi nationalism and, therefore, Sindhis holding high positions did, to some extent, find jobs for other Sindhis and facilitated matters for them in other ways as well. On the other hand, for the Mohajirs, the concept of 'Mohajir nationalism' was not considered important. In fact, many Mohajirs were completely indifferent towards it. And so the few Mohajirs in Pakistan's bureaucracy were of no use at all to the majority of their people.

9

The Founding of the APMSO

Background

As my involvement with the PNA decreased, I diverted myself back to the welfare of Mohajir students. As mentioned earlier, when I first entered the University of Karachi, I was struck by the sight of the many banners of student organizations which had been established on the basis of nationality, parochialism, and regionalism, and I had also observed that, on the basis of pressure-politics, these organizations could influence the three big student parties, the Islami Jamiat-e-Tulaba, the Progressives, and the Liberal Party. Thus they gained an advantage in obtaining admissions for their students and in finding accommodation for them in the hostel. During this time I had tried hard to convince these people to get rid of their parochial and regional biases.

But my appeals to activists and members of the various students' groups and unions to restrain themselves from bias fell on deaf ears although, overtly, they all pretended to agree with me. When I spoke to members of the Islami Jamiat-e-Tulaba they said, 'No, no, we are all Muslims and all brothers.' The Progressives claimed that their belief was that 'we are all human beings, and all human beings are equal.' But none demonstrated their beliefs in practice. Disappointed by this situation and, in the light of my experiences during the PNA campaign, I started a drive for building contacts and gaining support among the students. We could not hold our meetings in the B. Pharmacy department or in the Arts or Science faculties because we knew that the authorities would disapprove, so we held them clandestinely in the distant venue of the IBA (Institute of Business Administration). Gradually, the number of our sympathizers grew and soon we had about 150 members. Then, on 11 June 1978, we established our own organization by the name of All-Pakistan Mohajir Students' Organization (APMSO). In one of the meetings, I was elected Chairman of the new organization and Azeem Tariq, who is nowadays Chairman of the MQM, was elected General Secretary. Azeem was also a student of B. Pharmacy.

The organization had been launched but now the problem was of raising funds to print literature. Most of our members came from middle class families and paid for their education by giving tuitions, and were too poor to contribute financially. Azeem Tariq and I, too, gave tuitions to meet our expenses. Finally, we decided that each one of us would contribute Rs50, or at least Rs25 and with this sum we printed the organization's literature.

Reaction to the Launch of APMSO

When copies of the first pamphlet of APMSO were distributed, there was commotion in the university. The organizations based on regionalism and parochialism had been around for years and nobody had raised any objection about them. However, when the All-Pakistan Mohajir Students' Organization was launched, there was a hue and cry against it. It seemed as if the other students' organizations were shaken to the core. The Islami Jamiat-e-Tulaba's campaign was particularly vituperative because 70 to 80 per cent of the students in the university were Mohajirs, and the Jamiat was afraid that, if we were successful, they would lose the majority of their supporters. And, of course, without Mohajirs who would they have to make sacrifices for the Jamiat? Consequently, from the very first day of APMSO's existence, the Jamiat launched a vicious campaign against us and even issued *fatwas* condemning us. Yet, despite all opposition, our movement continued to exist and grow.

The details of the problems, anxieties, and grief we had to face to keep our movement alive are long and painful. Only my colleagues and I know how we managed to keep going; for, while all the other organizations enjoyed the sponsorship of one political party or another, ours was the only students' organization that had no powerful patron to safeguard its interests. Collecting donations for our organization was part of our daily routine, and it was through these means that we helped our party to move forward.

APMSO's Field of Activities

After establishing ourselves in the University of Karachi, we set up units in NED University, Urdu Science College, Dawood Engineering College, National College, Jinnah College, and Ship Owners' College. As the number of our units grew, so did our expenses. We needed more and more literature. Each of our members paid at least Rs25, but it was insufficient for our expenses. Other students' organizations at the University of Karachi spent enormous amounts. At the time of admissions at the university, each one of them spent vast sums of money on stalls, posters, pamphlets, and banners. It was not possible to be at par with them with our meagre resources. Hence, we finally decided to approach the public for donations. For this purpose we made teams. After lectures were over at the university, our teams would go to the different markets of Karachi and collect donations from the shops. Azeem Tariq and I would individually accompany one team or another. This became our daily routine.

Usually we would get only one or two rupees from each shop; some would say, '*Maaf karo*', as though we were beggars but we did not mind and continued on doggedly to the next shop. I have personally been given even paltry amounts like 10 or even 5 paisas to add to our fund. It was after the task of raising donations was completed that we would attend to our other responsibilities. After attending to them we would continue with our solicitations with friends and relatives for collection of funds for APMSO.

All team members kept a record of the contributions they received. Apart from the money collected in this manner, I also donated the income that I earned from my tuitions. Conveyance was a serious problem. I did not possess any private means of transport nor did any of my colleagues. All of us used to travel by bus. But, when our work became more demanding, the need for some form of transport to enable us to attend to our tasks became very acute. It was time for admissions at the University of Karachi by this time.

After the launch of APMSO, we had to work very hard for our first campaign during admission time. Hence we had to intensify our collection drive. We also had to get the posters and banners ready on time. Other students' organizations would set up their stalls at six or seven locations. We did what we could and, despite being an organization with meagre means, APMSO put up a performance as good as any of the others. Seeing this, our rivals started spreading propaganda against us: that we were receiving large amounts of funding and were flushed with money; that vested interests were sponsoring us. But we paid scant attention to such allegations.

It was the effort of every organization in those admission campaigns to attract and win over students who were seeking admissions. For this purpose they were all in possession of cars and motorcycles.

I have mentioned before that only those students were allotted rooms in the hostel that had the patronage of an influential organization and could thus operate from within the premises of the university. Since none of us had a room in the hostel, for our campaign we had to lug all the stuff for the stalls to the university in the morning, and then lug it all back with us in the evening. Naturally, we could not carry such a heavy load back and forth in buses.

10

The University of Karachi

Applying for a Room in the Hostel

Our application for a room in the university hostel was rejected. When we fought a legal battle for it, the room was eventually granted to us. But the very day after we got the room, boys from one student federation arrived and threw all our belongings out. We were astonished at this development and wondered how we could defend ourselves. We discovered that the boys from that student federation actually belonged to one of the three powerful organizations mentioned earlier and had acted on their instructions. Their intention was to try to obstruct us in every possible way. They knew that, if we found a place in the hostel, we would be able to work more effectively; that the more facilities we got the faster our organization would grow. We reported the incident to the university authorities. The hostel was closed for a few days, discussions were held, but we did not leave the hostel. I should also mention here that not only did the boys throw out our belongings, they also hauled me out of the room. Nevertheless, we did not lose courage and carried on our work.

The First Admissions Campaign

Each organization strived to establish its image in the eyes of the new entrants and attempted to prove that theirs was the most prominent body. Those organizations whose students possessed some means of conveyance would arrive at the university as early as 6 a.m. None of the APMSO members owned a motor vehicle and the university buses arrived late; so I asked my colleagues to take the minibus and come to the university as early as possible. We would set up our stalls at six or seven locations of the university. I brought the things we needed for the campaigning to the central stall and then distributed it to the other stalls. All this could not be done on foot; so I had brought a bicycle from my house and kept it in my hostel room. I would distribute the material to the various stalls on it and bring it back to my room in the hostel in the evening. Every evening, after we had collected everything from the stalls, we would place all the tables in one place and tie them together with iron chains. If we did not do this, the tables would get stolen during the night. I would begin my work of distributing our paraphernalia early enough to be able to finish it before the first buses arrived with the students. Many students would scoff at me for using a bicycle for my distribution work. 'What kind of movement do they expect to run on a bicycle? How can they help the Mohajirs if they can't even afford a motorbike?' were, no doubt, the sort of questions that rose in their minds.

However, I continued to work without giving in to feelings of inferiority or discouragement. We'd keep the stalls in place until one in the afternoon. Most of our members would leave for their homes after that. Even today there are people who are witness to the fact that I personally picked up the tables to take them to the place where they had to be chained. Having done that I would check all the items to make sure everything was there and nothing left behind. I would then prepare a press release and personally deliver it to the offices of all the newspapers. In addition, we had to prepare pamphlets and distribute them among the students. Other groups used to have their pamphlets printed beautifully but we could barely afford to have them cyclostyled. Anyhow, after delivering the news story to various newspaper offices, I would go to Burns Road to have the pamphlets cyclostyled and then walk to Empress Market from where I would take the bus for the university to return to the hostel.

In these circumstances we were in dire need of private transport. But neither the organization nor I had the money to afford even a motorbike. However, we had to do something to solve this transport issue; so I arranged to undertake two more tuitions in addition to the two that I was already giving. In this manner, I began to save some money. I also took a loan from my elder brother promising to pay it back in monthly instalments. A gentleman from my neighbourhood had a model 1969 Honda 50 motorbike which he sold to me in 1978 for

Rs2,900, assuring me that it had been driven by one person only and was in excellent condition. Trusting him, I bought the bike but, only a week later, its engine broke down. I had to wait for my tuition fee for the following month before I could get it fixed. But I must say that, from then on it worked excellently. In fact, it was not only used by me but also by other APMSO members. For six whole years, I ran the movement riding that bike and it never let me down. In pouring rain, when newer bikes stalled in the middle of the road, mine would keep running. I can never forget that 50 cc motorbike of mine which proved to be more faithful than many humans. It seemed to me that it understood me and was aware of all my travails and heartaches. Often it would carry me, along with two other companions, as late as 2 or 3 a.m., on the uneven roads of Korangi, or to Landhi, Malir, Drigh Road, New Karachi, and Orangi. Not only that, the three men riding it would be loaded with APMSO literature. No one can use a car the way we used that motorbike.

The Need for Funds

We continued our fund-raising routine of sending different teams to different parts of the city to collect donations. In this manner we managed to collect four to six hundred rupees every day. But these earnings were barely enough to meet our daily expenses and pay for the pamphlets we had to distribute practically every day.

It was a very arduous routine. Almost daily at about 2 p.m. or so we would leave the university on empty stomachs and would go to Burns Road, where we had the stencil cut for the pamphlet; got it cyclostyled; wrote the press release on a letter pad; and then delivered it to all the newspaper offices. I took on as much workload upon me as possible so that my colleagues did not feel over-burdened and, as a result, abandon us. However, that was precisely what happened. When we had begun our movement, we had about 150 people with us but we were soon left with only about 35. The work was so taxing that there were occasions when we were reduced to only a handful: Azeem, three or four others, and my-self. But at no stage did we lose courage.

However, in the course of our work, there were mo-ments which are etched in my memory and I can never forget them. Sometimes we did not have enough money. Therefore, we would first ask the salesman making the cyclostyle copies the amount needed for 2,000 or 4,000 pamphlets. We would then reduce the pamphlet in size and have it cyclostyled on half the paper originally planned so that instead of 2,000 pamphlets, 4,000 could be prepared from the same quantity of paper. Once we had paid for all this, we would be left with just enough for own bus ride back. Often, by this time, we would be suffering from pangs of hunger especially because we were on Burns Road, the famous food street, and could smell the tantalizing aroma of the delicious food of the roadside restaurants. It was not easy to ignore the aroma of *kababs*, *qorma*, and *nihari* and knowing that we were left with only about four rupees between us. Hence we would usually settle for a single *samosa* each followed by several glasses of water in an attempt to satisfy our seriously disgruntled stomachs.

My companions and I worked together as though we were one family. While it is true that, as a result of the very tough conditions, our numbers had greatly reduced but, of those who remained, about fifteen male and four female students, each one was loyal and dedicated to our cause. The following is an example of the steadfastness of my team at that time:

Once we had a meeting immediately after Eid. Since everybody knew that the biggest problem we faced was lack of funds, most of those present contributed all the *Eidi* (Eid gift in the form of cash) they had received while some gave half.

Some of the members suggested that we contact Mohajir businessmen to help us. I told them it would serve no purpose at all and none of them would help. My friends, however, insisted; their argument being for how long could we continue our expeditions into markets, streets and alleyways to collect only meagre amounts from small shopkeepers? I replied that we would continue to go to these places until every member of the Mohajir community became aware of our efforts and appreciated what we were doing for the Mohajirs. However, in order not to appear too unreasonable to my colleagues and create misunderstandings about my motives for sticking adamantly to my stand, I agreed to try their suggestion once.

Our subsequent efforts proved I was correct. Today I can challenge any prosperous Mohajir businessman or rich person to claim that he gave APMSO any financial help. We went to every affluent Mohajir, knocked at the door of their offices and homes, but they gave us nothing except advice. Some even told us, 'If you follow our directions and do as we say, we will finance you. The planning will be ours and you will do the work as you have been doing so far.' My companions and I immediately rejected such offers with the counter suggestion that they come out and work in the field with us and, since we needed the money, we would follow their instructions. This suggestion was not to their liking because they wanted to lay down the policy while sitting in their drawing rooms whereas we worked in the field. We also rejected other offers of financial help that had conditions attached to them.

11

Another Mohajir Organization

Thus we found that none of the affluent Mohajirs we met to solicit donations and cooperation had the least inclination to help us. Conversely some people tried to harm us. A well-known politician, whom I would rather not name, created a rival organization to ours, which he also named 'Mohajir'. When I arrived at the university during the admissions campaign, I found that banners of another organization of Mohajir students had been put up. It was called: 'The Mohajir Students' Organization', whereas ours was called: 'All-Pakistan Mohajir Students' Organization'. Their banners were everywhere, all around us.

When other students saw the banners of two new Mohajir organizations within a few months of each other, they, and especially a certain influential organization which was an adversary of ours, found a golden opportunity to spread propaganda against us. They and their stooges started saying, 'These Mohajirs can never remain united. In the space of a few days their group has split into two. There are now two Mohajir groups where only a short time ago there was one!' I tried to explain the situation to the students but the position as they saw it

was that the banners proved that there were two organizations. The gentleman who had founded the other
group was paying some boys to set up and run his stalls.
However, in my opinion, devotion and selflessness cannot
be bought with money. He had started the other group
out of arrogance and to spite us because we had rejected
his conditional offer of help. He wanted to put an end
to APMSO, but, instead, what transpired was that his
organization lasted no more than a month after which it
was never heard of again. However, I don't hold that
episode against him. We have put up with so many taunts,
criticisms, and accusations that forgiving and forgetting
have become second nature to us.

That was a definite detrimental result of this ill-
advised campaign. Otherwise I remember that often
when we went to the offices of wealthy Mohajirs, we
would send in a note and then have to wait three or four
hours in their reception rooms. We would be told that
the Sahib was busy in a meeting. After an endless wait,
when we would enquire again, we would be told that the
Sahib had left. 'But when did he leave?' we would ask
with astonishment, 'He could not have left the office
without passing through the reception.' And we'd be told
that he had left through a backdoor. So, in the end, we
gained nothing from the rich and influential Mohajirs
and, in the bargain, we lost a good deal of time. But on the
positive side my colleagues realized the reality of the
situation. I told them, 'This happens because we belong
to a poor and lower middle class. Had Altaf Hussain been

the son of a wealthy, well-placed man, he would not have to wait in the Sahib's office for so long. One phone call from his father would have brought the rich scrambling to his door, keen to dole out money.' I told my colleagues, 'There is no other way. We will have to go from street to street, from house to house, and put up with the taunts from some of the householders and shopkeepers. I do this myself too.' In such harsh conditions we carried on our work for APMSO. Thank God we remained steadfast and did not give up.

And now I will say something about the elections for the Students' Union. It was the first such election after the establishment of APMSO. For our meetings, we used to sit in a circle on the lawn of the Social Work, Pharmacy, or Journalism departments. Many students passing by would heap indescribable taunts, jeers, and derisive remarks upon us. Indeed it was the same wherever we went. What was most painful was that the vast majority of our detractors came from the Mohajir community itself. However, despite the abuse, we did not lose heart and carried on with our work.

Anyway, when the first election (after the birth of APMSO) for the university's Students' Union came around, all of us put our heads together and came to the conclusion that we would put up candidates for the elections also. However, the old problem of finances confronted us once again. We had no source of funding except collecting contributions. The members first reached into their own pockets. Some gave one hundred rupees, others fifty rupees. After that we embarked on our fund-raising campaign and redoubled our efforts in Karachi's market areas. When we'd go with our receipt books to the shopkeepers of Liaquatabad, Golimar, Nazimabad, Empress Market, Sarafa Bazaar, and Jama Cloth Market they would say to us, 'You came only a week ago to collect money, and now you are back so soon!' Perhaps they suspected we were misappropriating funds. However, some people did give five or ten rupees. I can't remember anybody giving a hundred rupees though, later, people did give more.

12

Taking Part in the Students' Union Elections

In the University of Karachi, where Mohajir students were in the majority among a student population of 10,000, the presidential candidate of our Mohajir organization which was waging a struggle for the Mohajirs received only 95 votes. It disheartened some of us but I told my colleagues not to get discouraged for the struggle in which we were engaged was not child's play. More difficult hurdles needed to be overcome and we needed to demonstrate that we were persevering. I give credit to my colleagues that they did not slacken and continued to work with as much enthusiasm as before. The following year, our organization got 900 votes. Thirty of our candidates for the positions of councillors were elected and for faculty representatives we won 1 out of 15 seats. Observing our success, a large number of Mohajir students, both male and female, joined us, and the APMSO began to fast gain popularity. Its position improved in other educational institutions as well and its numbers swelled.

The Islami Jamiat-e-Tulaba was most apprehensive at this state of affairs. They strongly feared that, if the

APMSO kept progressing at this pace, it would unquestionably have its own union elected in the University of Karachi the following year. Therefore, the Jamiat's Thunder Squad beat up some Mohajir students studying at the Urdu Science College and the University of Karachi. We displayed great fortitude on this occasion. During this period, on 1 February 1981, the admissions campaign began again in the University of Karachi. All the student organizations, including APMSO, put up their stalls. Among them were the Pakistan Liberal Students, Progressive Students' Organization, Jiye Sindh Students' Federation, Baloch Students' Organization, Pakhtun Students' Federation, Punjabi Students' Association, and Islami Jamiat-e-Tulaba. During the campaign, not only are new entrants guided, but also admission forms are provided to them to save them the hassle of standing in long queues in front of banks waiting to pay their admission fee. For the convenience of newcomers, the various organizations also print pamphlets in which the details of the different departments and the admission procedure are explained.

It became apparent during this campaign that the largest crowd of students gathered at the APMSO stall. The rush was so great at our stall that queues had to be made. The other stalls were more or less empty, even though students could have easily obtained their admission forms from any one of them, but it seemed that the entrants were determined to obtain their forms from our stall even though it meant waiting in queues.

This showed the preference of the students and, *ipso facto*, the organization they were likely to support.

Observing this situation, the Islami Jamiat-e-Tulaba sent for members of their Thunder Squad from all over Karachi and, on 3 February they launched an armed assault on all APMSO stalls. They attacked our workers with firearms and also knives. All the stalls were ransacked and set on fire. The female students stationed at the stalls had their *dupattas* pulled from their heads and were insulted in other disgraceful ways. Their bags were snatched from them. The money received from selling the admission forms was forcibly seized. APMSO flags were torn down and stamped upon.

They also attacked me with deadly intentions and badly injured many of my companions who were trying to protect me. My colleagues, both male and females bravely made a circle around me and thus I remained unhurt. However, I remained there till the end. When the attackers saw the APMSO workers wounded and bleeding, they left shouting slogans as they went. After the attack I took my wounded workers to the hospital. Azeem Ahmed Tariq, then the General Secretary, received a knife wound in his hand. Indeed the barbarism demonstrated on that day was an unforgettable chapter in the history of the University of Karachi.

When we lodged an FIR, instead of arresting the attackers, the police browbeat and threatened us. They put pressure on us to withdraw our report. It was strange and unfortunate that victims of violence were not allowed to complain. Since there was censorship in the country in those days, newspapers did not publish our story. In any case, even in ordinary times, we were subjected to stepmotherly treatment.

Because the government of the day was openly supporting the Jamiat, we were not even given a copy of the FIR despite our requests. The university administration dared not show any sympathy towards us even if they wanted to. However, the Vice Chancellor, Mr Tirmizi, did come to the hospital to enquire about our wounded workers.

13

Educational Institutions

We had established units in NED University, Urdu Science College, Ship Owners' College, Jinnah College and other educational institutions in addition to the University of Karachi. In all these places, our workers were being pressured to stop working for APMSO. After the 3 February 1981 incident, the Jamiat threatened those in all the other educational institutions where we had established our stalls. Using firearms, they barred APMSO workers from entering the University of Karachi and Urdu Science College. By then I had completed B. Pharmacy and was a student of M. Pharmacy, but the situation became so menacing that I was forced to leave the university.

The situation had deteriorated to the extent that our workers could not enter the university without being subjected to violence. We could not defend ourselves against our adversaries because they had no shortage of weapons. By no means were our workers deficient in courage but, being unarmed, they were no match for the Jamiat workers who possessed sten-guns, revolvers, axes and staffs.

On 3 February, after our wounded workers had been provided with medical assistance, we sat down at night to think over the new developments. I said to my companions, 'What are we to do now? Devotion to one's cause, no matter how deep, does not equip one to face an armed enemy. How can one work in such circumstances?'

But despite those difficult times, all my colleagues told me, 'No matter what the circumstances, we will carry on our struggle.'

Once again I visited Karachi's elite and told them, 'You are Mohajirs and we are struggling for the rights of Mohajirs. See how our opponents have treated us in the educational institutions. You must help us.' But I am sorry to say that none of them was prepared to support us.

Finally, I was obliged to gather my colleagues and tell them:

We have worked for the Mohajir cause for three years, from 1978 to 1981, at the University of Karachi and other educational institutions, but our enemies could not tolerate the success we achieved and they are now openly terrorizing us. We lack the resources to counter their terrorism nor is anybody prepared to help us. So now we will have to fold up the Mohajir flag we hoisted at the University of Karachi and other educational institutions; we will have to pack away the Mohajir name. We have tried our best to build a Mohajir institution and work through it but, now, how can we stand up to armed might?

I can never forget that scene as long as I live. I was speaking in a meeting which we held in a house in Federal

B Area. When I said that we would have to fold up the Mohajir flag and wind up our work every one of my colleagues in the room began to sob. They wept as people weep when they lose a close relative. My words struck such grief into their hearts that some banged their heads against the walls so hard that blood flowed out. Seeing their distress I asked them, 'What do you want to do?'

'We want to work for the Mohajir cause at any price,' was their answer.

'All right,' I said, 'if that is what you want to do, we will carry on. But since they have barred us from setting foot in the university and other educational institutions, we will now go into every street, every neighbourhood and every city to spread the Mohajir name and work for the Mohajir cause.'

After Banishment from Educational Institutions

Even before 3 February 1981, we used to hold our meetings in different areas of the city. But, in those days our work was aimed only at the students' level. Now we were prevented from entering educational institutions. However, though a door had closed upon us, another had opened!

We started holding our meetings in the lanes and alleyways of different parts of the city and our units were established in areas of Karachi. Earlier, it was only students who joined us; now people from different walks of life began to support APMSO. Our units started gaining strength. Even if we held a meeting in an area only at the level of its unit, the number of people who flocked to it exceeded that of many political parties' major meetings.

All of us came from poor or middle class backgrounds and we had no influence either with the elite or with the press. Even our large and well-attended meetings were never reported in the newspapers. Time and again we sent invitations to the newspapers, appealed to them, and I would personally request all of them to attend our meetings but they gave us no importance at all.

Moreover, besides Karachi, we established our units in several other cities and towns of Sindh and began to tour the whole province. In those days our organization still went by the name of APMSO.

14

The Launching of
Mohajir Quami Movement

A large number of young people had joined APMSO in addition to students. We, too, had completed our university education and were no longer students. Therefore, we decided that a separate organization for the Mohajir cause was needed for the general public. Many other people also insisted that we should have such an organization. So it came about that, on 18 March 1984, we launched the Mohajir Quami Movement (MQM).

The MQM gained support among older people, too, but their numbers were less than those of young men and women. The older people who joined us usually belonged to the poor or the lower middle class. They, too, attended our meetings, worked with us, and contributed towards the movement. However, since the youth frequently found themselves beset by problems, their numbers increased more rapidly. To this day, no prominent personality or member of the elite has allied himself with us because usually such people prefer to associate themselves with the more prominent organizations which would enhance their status. Since nobody could expect such elevation by joining us, they did not bother about us. But we didn't need them; middle class and poor people flocked to us and, so, despite the myriad problems we faced, the MQM grew at a fast pace.

In 1986, when political parties started to hold public meetings, our workers insisted on holding a meeting at Nishtar Park. I told them that, though the idea of holding a meeting in Nishtar Park was very tempting, to do so would require much organization and large sums of money. But our supporters averred that, even if they had to work day and night, they would hold this meeting and make it a success. Our main problem was, of course, funds. We held a meeting of our three Karachi units and other units from various cities and discussed the matter. Every unit gave us a donation target. We decided to announce the date of the meeting only after the donation targets had been met and we had the required amount in our kitty. I give credit to all the workers and regional office-bearers who met their target by the stipulated date. Only after this did we announce our meeting in Nishtar Park. Even then the media gave us no importance and, prior to the meeting, we did not get a tenth of the coverage that was given to other organizations.

Most people did not take the MQM seriously but the eight-year struggle of our colleagues bore fruit and, on 8 August 1986, this was demonstrated at the Nishtar Park meeting, which was attended by hundreds of thousands of people and must have been a rare event in Pakistan's history. To my knowledge, it was the first meeting in which there were torrential rains but, even as it poured, voices shouting *'Nara-e-Mohajir, Jeeay Mohajir'* grew louder. The meeting proved to be even better organized than many historic meetings. The heart's desire of my colleagues came true and the name 'Mohajir' was finally in the public eye. It was only after this meeting that the public suddenly became aware that there was an organization called the MQM and that is the reason why many people are of the impression that the MQM came up in just two years. This was the first time the MQM was mentioned on the front page of newspapers and, unfortunately, in our society an organization is recognized only when it is given prominence by the press even though some of these recognized organizations may be confined only to the drawing room or all their workers and office-bearers can fit into one taxi. Few people who lived in houses as small as mine and my colleagues' could have started a new organization and then taken it to the level to which we took the MQM. In the beginning, our small houses were the reason why we were given no importance.

The Importance of MQM

After that massive meeting all the elements who were the enemies and exploiters of Mohajirs became actively hostile towards us. They felt that, if the Mohajirs became united and organized, they (the enemies and exploiters) would face a huge problem since our slogan was that those inhabitants of Sindh who earn their income here, spend it here, do not send it elsewhere and, who live and die in Sindh, have the first right on Sindh. People found this unpalatable even though we clearly stated that our movement was not against the Punjabis or the Pakhtuns; it was just a movement for our own rights. We say to our Punjabi and Pakhtun compatriots:

Why do you believe that, by making our demands, we are showing hostility towards you? You should compel those of your regional leaders who come to Karachi and hold meetings here to wage a struggle to establish industries in (their own) Punjab and Frontier and work for an environment that can provide livelihood for their people, who would then not have to leave their families and come all the way to Karachi to seek their livelihood. We talk of their rights as well as ours. We talk of the poor and the oppressed in those parts, too, and not just in Karachi.

When the other political and religio-political parties saw that, while we gained, they were suffering losses, they started saying, 'Mohajirs are not a nationality; it is wrong to divide on the basis of nationality; discrimination on the basis of language should be ended; the concept of "Mohajir" is wrong in the light of Islamic law, etc., etc.' And these were the very same parties for whom the Mohajirs had given untold sacrifices in the past. These parties had never condemned parties with Pakhtun, Punjabi, Sindhi, Baloch, Seraiki, Kashmiri, or Gilgiti as part of their names but, regarding the reference to 'Mohajir' in our name, they could not stop raising all sorts of objections against this. Never had they found the

concept of a Pakhtun, Punjabi, Sindhi, or Baloch party
wrong in the light of Islamic law nor had they ever proclaimed views about the fallibility of four nationalities
but, as soon as there was talk of a Mohajir nationality, all
their philosophy, all their *fatwas* came into play. This
showed how much sympathy these parties actually had
for Mohajirs. Even though the Mohajirs had supported
them and had rendered sacrifices for them in the past,
they could not bear to see them united. Thus they turned
their guns on us. They began to level false accusations
against us that, we were enemies of the country, that
we were separatists, saboteurs, and agents of foreign
countries. Quite simply, talking of rights for the Mohajirs
was nothing short of treason. Despite these strange
accusations levelled at us, it goes to the credit of my
colleagues that they remained steadfast to the Mohajir
cause.

After the Karachi meeting, the Mohajirs of Hyderabad expressed the desire to hold an MQM meeting in
Hyderabad. We made the same arrangements as we did
in Karachi and it was decided that, on 31 October 1986,
a meeting would be held at Pucca Qila in Hyderabad.
But, as I said before, our unity and popularity was
intolerable to Mohajir haters and exploiters. On 31
October 1986, while our procession was marching
peacefully towards Hyderabad, it was attacked at
Sohrab Goth with Kalashnikovs and rifles and some of
our colleagues were killed. As we proceeded further,
more of our people got killed at the Hyderabad Market.

The last words of those who were killed in the firing were, 'Our message to the centre is that the meeting should be made completely successful.' Many of our friends uttered this message before they died.

On the day of the meeting I had arrived in Hyderabad at 8.30 a.m. in order to oversee the arrangements. At the venue, when I was informed that our processions had been fired upon and people had been killed, there was a huge crowd of half a million people gathered there. However, I didn't utter a word about this tragedy throughout my speech. If I had done so, the crowd would have become incensed and violence would have erupted.

Never before in the history of the city had there been a crowd like this. Their enthusiasm had to be seen to be believed. The rickshaw drivers were giving free rides to those who came to the meeting. Restaurants were providing free meals to the gathering. However, slowly, as some of the people from the procession that had been attacked reached the venue, news of the armed assault got around. During my speech, people repeatedly asked me to talk about the Sohrab Goth incident but I kept telling them to wait until our colleagues, whose responsibility it was to find out the details gave their report. I had to say this because, if I had told them about the young men who had been killed and wounded in the two attacks, the crowd of half a million could have gone out of control. I could not even call for a *Fateha Khawani* for our slain colleagues. The other leaders of the MQM and I had to restrain our feelings though we were overwhelmed with grief and anger.

After the meeting, I held a press conference in Hyderabad. We had been informed that there was a strong reaction of our people to the attack in Karachi and it had spread. We decided that Azeem Ahmed Tariq (Chairman, MQM) would participate in the funeral prayers for the victims of the shooting in Hyderabad while I would go to Karachi to attend the funeral prayers there and try to persuade the Mohajirs to remain peaceful.

At 7 p.m., as soon as the press conference was over, I left for Karachi. Before I left, I announced that those who had come from Karachi for the meeting must go back via the National Highway and Thatta, and nobody should take the Super Highway route. I gave these instructions specifically so that nobody would retaliate when they passed Sohrab Goth which lies on the Super Highway. I was also returning via Thatta when I was arrested at Ghagghar Phatak along with hundreds of my colleagues. All kinds of cases were registered against us. On the other hand not one of the assailants was arrested although, the names of many of them were published in the papers and mentioned in FIRs. What actually happened was that, when I was released and the cases against me were withdrawn, the cases against the attackers who were present were also withdrawn although, the cases against me and my colleagues were entirely false.

While I was still in jail, the tragic Aligarh Colony and Qasba Colony episode occurred which I think was the worst incident of its kind in the history of Pakistan. There was nothing I could do but pray to God and cry out to Him.

After my release, the first thing I did was to go to the houses of each of the martyrs of Karachi and Hyderabad, condole with their families, and recite *fateha* for the departed ones. I was arrested on the night of 31 October 1986 and released on 24 February 1987. The enthusiasm with which the people greeted me and showered their affection on me after my release when I toured their areas is my most treasured memory. This enraged my opponents even more. Their plan had been to crush the MQM through these tactics.

Man makes momentous decisions on this earth believing himself to be God. But there is just one God, and our lives rest only in His power. He is ruler of all and the most powerful.

Thus, during those years, we faced so many difficulties, we went through very bad times, and were the victims of violence and oppression but, in the end, everybody saw that the elaborate planning of our exploiters and detractors to extirpate the Mohajir organization from the pages of history failed completely. We have emerged successful. The historic success of the 'Haq Parast' (truth worshipers) Mohajirs in the 1987 local bodies' elections in Karachi and Hyderabad remains unequalled.

Part II

Notes on Important Issues and the Mohajir Movement

15

The Steadfastness of the Mohajirs

A case was made against me for stealing the cap and belt of a policeman in the Korangi police station. This is one example of the ridiculous cases that were brought against me. But the world saw that, in spite of the oppression Mohajirs had to put up with, they did not lose courage. They proved that they were the sons and daughters of those who knew how to die but did not know how to bow down; and who suffered brutality for the crime of demanding Pakistan. Praise be to the mothers, sisters, brothers, and the martyrs. Speaking of martyrs, I would say that God accepted the offering of our martyrs' blood because they did not offer those sacrifices for greed or for personal gains. The blood of the 31 October martyrs of Sohrab Goth and Hyderabad was innocent blood. After that came the next bloodbath at Aligarh and Qasba colonies when innocent youths, the elderly, and women and children were gunned down by the drug mafia. Theirs, too, was innocent blood. It was not only the drug mafia that shed innocent blood but also the police who came into our localities and opened indiscriminate fire upon the people—aiding in their massacre instead of coming to their rescue and protection. They even fired at pedestrians passing by. Again, on 31 March 1988, the police opened fire at the funeral procession of a woman killing the deceased's son and wounding four others. Many of our brothers were martyred by the police but no court of justice ever sentenced them nor was any policeman ever sacked. Such is the justice of our land. Exposed to all these atrocities, open fraud, and barbarism, what is a Pakistani forced to think? He will wonder, 'Who are we that we are being treated in this way?'

Today, people ask, 'Why has this Mohajir organization come into being? What problems were the Mohajirs suffering from?'

I ask all my Pakistani compatriots, when Aligarh and Qasba colonies were attacked early in the morning after announcements were made from loudspeakers in mosques and for six hours violence continued unabated; where were the administration, the institutions of justice, and the guardians of the public's life and property? Why did they remain silent witnesses to this barbarism? Why hasn't even a single person responsible for the massacre in Aligarh and Qasba colonies ever been apprehended? Is this justice? Isn't this proof of bias? I challenge anyone to produce a single instance where the MQM perpetrated such barbarism on any community.

It is a misfortune that, instead of censuring the activities of the drug mafia and exploitative groups, the incident has been given a different colour. To conceal the brutality of this act and shield the oppressor, people now say: 'What is the matter with us Pakistanis that we fight among ourselves? A brother kills a brother; a Muslim murders a Muslim?' What I want to know is, is it right to call the brutal killers of the unarmed people of Aligarh and Qasba colonies, 'brothers', or 'Muslims'? In my view, this incident was the worst and the most tragic of its kind in the history of Pakistan. How can a 'Muslim' shoot other unarmed Muslims with his Kalashnikov or sten-gun? What kind of 'Muslims' were they who snatched an infant from her mother's lap and threw it into the fire? Can a Muslim treat another Muslim so brutally? And can such happenings be underplayed and termed as 'a quarrel among brothers'? Can a 'peace march' make amends for such deeds?

I want to make it clear that this was no 'brothers' quarrel', but a brazen armed attack on a settled neigh-bourhood. In our long struggle we never resorted to such violence. We respect all communities. Our struggle was never against a particular community, whether Punjabis or Pakhtuns or anyone else. We were struggling only for our rights. We wanted only to retrieve our rights that had been snatched from us.

It was unfortunate that our intellectuals, too, turned against the Mohajirs. Their pens became busy but only to condemn the Mohajirs. I would like to point out to them that, if the impressions some of them have project-ed about us are true, then why do people continue to genuinely come in flocks to vote for us?

The attack on Shah Faisal Colony, too, was carried out openly. Thirty-two police trucks were present at the time of the attack but not a single attacker was arrested. Pakistanis should think about this: Does the MQM want clashes? Does the MQM cause and bring about the clashes? From the beginning, an exploitative group backed by certain well-known violent elements has been trying to crush the MQM and the Mohajirs and they are the ones who commit mayhem, aided by the drug mafia and the bureaucracy under a conspiracy. As I said before, God has accepted the blood of our martyrs. Those colleagues who were maimed by enemy bullets—some lost an arm, others a leg—their sacrifices also have not gone in vain. The efforts of my colleagues and the Mohajir workers who toiled hard were made fruitful by the Grace of God. The conspiracies that were hatched against us failed, with God's assistance, and the world was witness to the fact that God upholds truth and crushes falsehood. If truth had not been on our side, we would not have been granted such a magnificent success in the local bodies' elections despite the enemy propaganda, brutality, and innumerable obstacles that were placed in our path. All our office-bearers, units, and workers remained steadfast. Not a single individual deserted us during this critical period. This is a record unique to the MQM. No other party can claim a similar record of loyalty. Does this not prove that every single individual in the MQM is completely sincere? The reason for this is that Truth is with the MQM and we are working towards an honest goal.

16

Local Bodies' Elections, the Law and Order Situation in Karachi, and the Drug Mafia

The local bodies' elections proved to be a kind of referendum in which the Mohajir public gave the MQM their mandate. By bringing victory to the 'Haq Parast' candidates, they demonstrated their full confidence in the MQM. Some political parties claimed that the MQM was an organization of non-serious young people but, during the local bodies' elections, they saw, like everybody else, that men and women, some as old as ninety years, stood in the long queues to vote for the MQM. Nobody can say now that the MQM is 'an organization only of non-serious youth.' It has now been proved that the MQM has won the hearts of every Mohajir mother, father, sister, and brother. Even innocent Mohajir children go about their neighbourhood and streets shouting the slogan of '*Jeeay Mohajir*'. This is proof of the fact that we have the help and support of God and that Truth was, and is, on our side.

* * *

Some time ago, a house was raided in Orangi and some equipment was recovered. The next day newspapers carried headlines that said, 'a house in Orangi was raided and a bomb-making factory found.' The news story also mentioned that, when the police raided the house, *parathas* were being fried there. Isn't it ridiculous that *parathas* were being fried in a factory meant for making weapons? The truth was that a poor man's house was raided when his wife was making *parathas* for breakfast!

What more can I say except that the tyranny of our oppressors knows no bounds. In Shah Faisal Colony, Mohajir settlements were torched in the presence of policemen. Shops were set on fire. The police did not apprehend the saboteurs but, when the Mohajirs tried to defend themselves, the police fired on them.

The police have devised a formula for describing these incidents. They call it 'a clash between two rivals'. Actually, it is not a conflict between two rivals; in these cases there has always been an aggressor and victims. The victims are arrested if they try to defend themselves. What kind of justice is this? How can a murderer and his victim be meted out the same treatment? This cruelty continues to this day.

* * *

Most of the blame for ruining the peace and tranquillity of Karachi falls on the drug mafia. There are others with

Mohtarm Nazir Hussain (Late),
father of Mr Altaf Hussain,
Karachi. 24 May 1964.

Mohtarma Khursheed Begum
(Late), mother of Mr Altaf
Hussain, Karachi. 24 May 1964.

Mr Altaf Hussain with his father, Mr Nazir Hussain, mother, Khursheed
Begum, elder sisters, Sajida Begum and Saliha Begum, elder brothers Iqbal
Hussain and Abrar Hussain, younger brother, Asrar Hussain, and cousin,
Saeed Qureshi. Government Quarters, Jahangir Road. Karachi, May 1964.

The saga of Mr Altaf Hussain's childhood in the form of photographs.

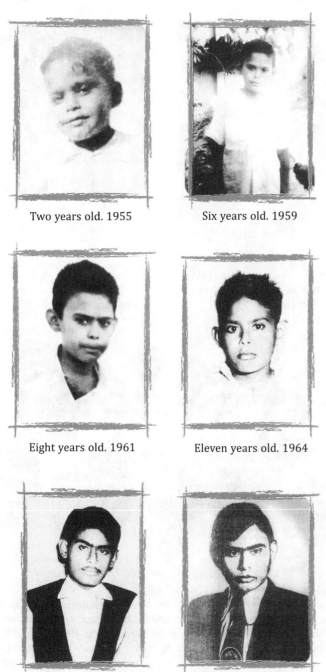

Two years old. 1955

Six years old. 1959

Eight years old. 1961

Eleven years old. 1964

Sixteen years old. 1969

Nineteen years old. 1972

After obtaining admission at the National College, Mr Altaf Hussain
(extreme right) with his brother, Asrar Hussain, and cousin,
Saeed Qureshi. 1969.

With APMSO members displaying the first flag of the organization.
Karachi, 1978.

On his way to the University of Karachi. 1978.

With his companions after a meeting at the IBA Block, University of Karachi. 1978.

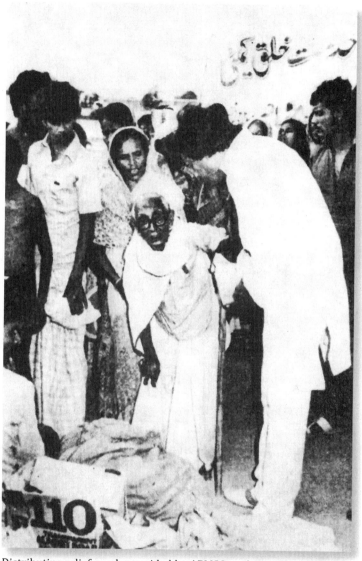

Distributing relief goods provided by APMSO at the various camps of
refugees coming from East Pakistan. 5 July 1979.

Arrested and sentenced to nine months' imprisonment by the Martial
Law Court. October 1979.

On his release from imprisonment; jubilant workers are gathered
around him. Karachi, 28 April 1980.

Dr Farooq Sattar receiving a medal
from Mr Altaf Hussain for his
outstanding performance as a
member of APMSO. Karachi, 1981.

At the function of the third anniversary of APMSO.
Karachi, 11 June 1981.

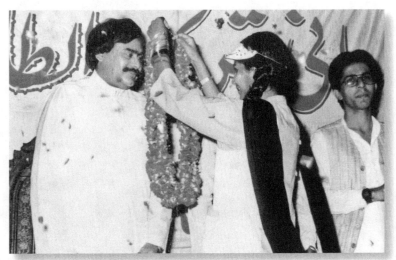
Being garlanded by a worker at the annual function of APMSO at
Al-Madina Hall, North Nazimabad. Karachi, 1983.

Busy in his studies in Chicago, Illinois,
USA, 1984.

Sorting pictures for newspapers of photo-section at MQM Headquarters. Karachi, 1986.

Offering prayers at the home of the martyrs of Aligarh and Qasba Colonies. Karachi, 1986.

Mr Altaf Hussain in Rajasthani turban (above) and a Sindhi *ajrak* and *topi* (below) during his tour of interior Sindh. 1986.

On his visit to Mirpurkhas. 1986.

MQM's first public convention at Nishtar Park. Karachi, 8 August 1986.

Checking the attendance record of workers at Liaquatabad Sector. 1987.

With Sindhi nationalist leader, Mr Abdul Wahid Aresar
extreme right. 1987.

Addressing the members of Mirpurkhas Bar during his tour of
interior Sindh. 1987.

Enquiring about the tragic incident of Aligarh Colony and Qasba Colony, Orangi Town. Karachi, January 1987.

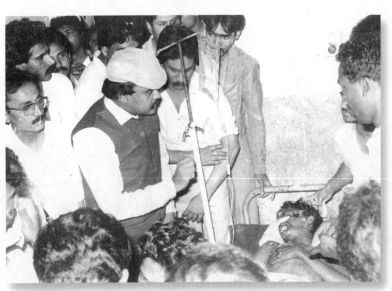

Enquiring about the health of a worker who faced racial oppression. January 1987.

'Meet the Press' at the Karachi Press Club. 1 February 1987. With Imran
Farooq and Mahmood Ali Asad (President, Karachi Press Club).

A group photograph on the occasion of the marriage ceremony of Mr
Altaf Hussain's younger brother, Mr Asrar Hussain. The bridegroom with
Mr Altaf Hussain, Mr Azeem Ahmed Tariq, Mr Mujib-ur-Rehman, and
others. Karachi, 16 August 1987.

Mr Ghulam Ishaq Khan, President of
Pakistan, meeting with Mr Altaf Hussain at
the State Guest House. Karachi, 1988.

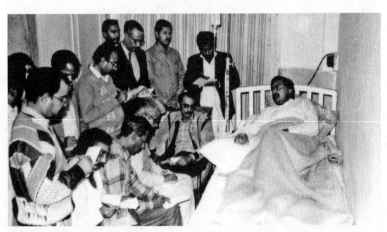

At a press conference with senior journalists during his illness,
Civil Hospital. Karachi, 13 January 1988.

Participating in the activities of the 'Hafta-e-Safai' (Cleanliness Week) Campaign. Karachi, 9–16 September 1988.

Offering prayers for the martyrs of the Karachi riots. October 1988.

Presenting the Holy Quran to Mohtarma Benazir Bhutto.
21 November 1988.

A group photograph on the occasion of the marriage ceremony of Mr Altaf
Hussain's nephew, Mr Shahid Hussain. Mr Altaf Hussain, Saira Aslam, M.
Aslam, M. Sami, Sualeh Sami, Tahira Khateeb, Nasir Hussain, and Tayyaba
Saeed. Karachi, 1988.

Addressing massive crowds on two different occasions. Karachi, 1988.

Mr Altaf Hussain. 1988.

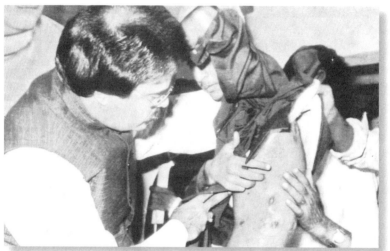

Looking at the injuries of a worker during his visit to a hospital, Karachi.

Enquiring about the health of MQM workers injured in a terrorist attack.
Mr Azeem Ahmed Tariq, Dr Imran Farooq along with I.G., Sindh and
Commissioner, Karachi.

Arriving on his famous Honda 50 at the 'Dhanak Mela' at the University of Karachi organized by APMSO.

Inaugurating the Coffin Carrier and Ambulance Service of
Khidmat-e-Khalq Committee, Karachi.

Briefing women workers regarding the preparation of the COP procession, MQM Headquarters.

With Azeem Ahmed Tariq, Tariq Javed, and Ahmed Saleem Siddiqui on the occasion of Qaumi Mela at T-Ground, Azizabad, Karachi.

different interests but the interests of some of these are also tied to those of the drug mafia. They want to see discord and conflict in Karachi so that the drug mafia can do what it likes. The English newspaper, *Daily News*, once published a comprehensive list of all the people involved in drug trafficking also mentioning the names of those who ran dens and gave their addresses as well as other details such as which police station's precincts each den was located in. If the administration and bureaucracy had wanted to take action against them, they had all the information they needed. But, to this day, it is not known what action, if any, was taken against these drug dens. If the drug mafia continues to benefit from such lapses and if the police continues to be a party to oppression, the peace and tranquillity of this city will never be realized.

I would like to remind readers about the statement I issued from Karachi Central Jail after the victory of the 'Haq Parasts':

> Today we forgive and forget everything that has happened in the past and I instruct the 'Haq Parast' councillors that, starting from today, they must demonstrate that they are not the representatives of the Mohajirs only; they must serve our Punjabi, Pakhtun, and other compatriots even-handedly, just as they would serve Mohajirs.

After my release, I am sorry to say that no positive response was given to the points I raised in the 'Meet the Press' programme at the Karachi Press Club. I had said that we would serve the Punjabis and the Pakhtuns living in our settlements just as we treat the Mohajirs. But some religio-political parties began a propaganda against us with the intention of spreading hatred against me and the MQM among the Punjabis and the Pakhtuns. Furthermore, when Abdul Wali Khan came to Karachi, the government immediately sent him back in order that we are not able to have a meeting. We were keen to hold a discussion with Wali Khan as he was the undisputed leader of the Pakhtuns. One can't say why the government was averse to our meeting. Similarly, we stated that we were prepared to speak to patriotic and respected Punjabis but would, on no account, parley with any member of the drug mafia even if he was a Mohajir.

17

Jail Experiences

As related before, I have been arrested three times so far.

– I –

The first time was on 14 August 1979. On this day I was arrested from Quaid-i-Azam's mausoleum for demonstrating in favour of bringing the stranded Mohajirs from the former East Pakistan (now Bangladesh) to Pakistan. At that time I was the Chairman of APMSO. We had held a peaceful demonstration, and afterwards, when our procession reached Capri Cinema, we were surrounded by the Frontier Constabulary. The police arrested me and, before being thrown into the police van, I was beaten so hard and for so long that I could no longer tell which part of my body was being struck. The distance between Capri Cinema and the Soldier Bazaar police station hardly takes five minutes but the van was driven on a round-about route for an hour before we got to our destination and, during this time, the men of the Frontier Constabulary continued to hit me with sticks. Finally, when we reached the police station, I was locked up without food or water.

Many other people, including Afaq Shahid and Haseeb Hashmi, were arrested at the same time. The martial law government registered all kinds of cases against me. We were all thrown into the same lock-up which was filled beyond its capacity. There was no question of lying down; there was hardly place to sit. The open toilet was overflowing and bugs were crawling out of it. We found a piece of sackcloth and tried to pick up the insects with it and throw them back into the open toilet from which they would creep out again. We stayed there for three days under these conditions.

When we had been pulled out of the van at the lock-up, no part of my body was free from pain and my head was swollen from the blows I had received. In the lock-up I discovered that my whole body was blue from the beatings. These beatings later resulted in kidney problems. Anyway, these are minor hardships that have to be suffered when one is running a movement; they have to be endured with fortitude.

Three days later, tied with ropes, we were confined within the worst cell block, popularly known as 'Kerratin'. There were neither sheets nor blankets there. Having to remain awake for three nights and exhausted, I was not able to lie down because of the pain and injury to my back. Even sitting down was painful. Yet, I was so exhausted that I collapsed on the bare floor but was unable to rest my head on the ground due to the pain.

Finally, I placed my shoes under my head and used them as a pillow and somehow managed to pass the night that way.

The next morning, when I woke up, my body was suffering from extreme pain. I desperately wanted some tea to assuage my suffering. The clerk at 'Kerratin' had a stick in his hand with which he answered all our questions. After a short while I saw that a man with a steaming kettle was filling up cups of the inmates. I didn't have any vessel so I borrowed a broken plastic cup from a man sitting close by and the man with the kettle served me. When I took a sip I thought with surprise that they gave very salty tea in jail. The second sip cleared up the mystery: the 'tea' was actually a watery, lentil soup.

Later, I was sent to the common criminals' block, known as 'Chakkar'. After about a month and a half, I was shifted to the political prisoners' block number 2/5, even though I should have been sent there on the first day. However, I was glad that I had seen how the prisoners in 'Kerratin' and 'Chakkar' were treated and got to know their problems. 'Chakkar' is that part of the jail where prisoners are kept before the hearing. While I was there I got a chance to hear from the prisoners about the various ways in which they were taken to the prison and why they had been forced to commit crimes.

On 12 October 1979, the martial law government sentenced me to nine months' hard labour with imprisonment and five lashes. While I was in prison, the authorities offered me several deals which would have lightened my sentence but I refused them all and served the full nine months.

The High Court challenged the verdict of the martial law court. The bench allowed the nine months' incarceration but revoked the lashes. Before the lashes were cancelled, I used to watch other prisoners being lashed, in order to prepare myself for the lashings.

– II –

The second time I was arrested by the Karachi police on 31 October 1986 when I was on my way back to Karachi from our historic meeting in Hyderabad after the tragic incidents of Sohrab Goth and Hyderabad bazaar. At the time of the arrest, the District Magistrate of Karachi East, Ashfaq Memon, SSP East, Altaf Ali Khan, the SDM (I don't remember his name), SHO Tajammal Hussain, and a heavy contingent of police were present. Before Ghaggar Phatak, we were taken to Khokhrapar police station, or perhaps to some other police station, and then we were deposited at the Kalaboard police station. At first we were not treated too badly. But once we were put in the lock-up, we were confronted by the same conditions as we had been at the Soldier Bazaar police station in 1979. The toilet was choked and overflowing. All my cell mates felt sick because of the foul smell.

Two days later, some people came and took me and my cell mates with them in a car to an unknown destination. Later, I learned that we had been taken to the interrogation cell of the CIA. We were confined in a tiny room where we were guarded by gunmen with their guns pointing at us. There I was treated as though I was some dangerous terrorist. Observing all this, I wondered what I had done to deserve this treatment. After all, this was my own country and these, my own people. I asked myself these questions and then answered them myself:

> Because this movement has sprung up from poor people, the exploitative class will never want to see it succeed. The Mohajirs have been subjected to injustices for the past forty years and those who deprived us of our rights would never want us to regain them. That is the reason why they treat me in this way and none other. So I had better be prepared to bear all the pain they are going to inflict.

Sometime later, I was taken out of the cell and put in another that was dusty and dirty. I had never seen so many mosquitoes in a room before. I was provided with a filthy rug to sleep on which I had to dust and clean with my hands for a long time. I had not slept for the previous three nights which I had spent in the lock-up and before that I had been up for three nights in connection with the preparations for the meeting in Hyderabad. Hence, by this time I had been awake for six nights. As soon as I tried to sit on the rug, I was ordered to not sit down and keep pacing up and down the room I was forced to continuously keep pacing for seven days in that tiny CIA cell without once being allowed to sit down. My feet had swollen and the pain in my kidneys was dreadful. I asked them why they were doing this to me but received no answer. Officers from different agencies would come there and take me outside the room at intervals. They would speak to me, sometimes in gentle tones, but, at other times, their language would be full of filthy and unrepeatable abuses. I was given a cigarette only when I was taken for interrogation. Perhaps they wanted to find out if I was addicted to some drug.

The interrogation unit would normally ask me questions such as: 'Who sponsors you?' 'Who helps you?' 'How much did you spend on the Nishtar Park meeting?' 'Where did that money come from?' etc. In reply to their questions, I told them the facts but they would not believe me. I told them, 'We collect the money we need from the streets; we go from door to door.' And it is a fact that the way the MQM collects its money from the streets and, has never been adopted by any political or religio-political party in Pakistan before which was why my interrogators refused to believe me.

Seven days went by in excruciating pain and misery. On the seventh day, I fell unconscious. When I regained consciousness, I thought they might be more merciful but I was ordered to start pacing up and down again. I pleaded to them that I could not walk any more but they would not listen. The result was that, after a little while I fell unconscious again. This happened three times. Finally, I told a soldier who was on duty there to call his officer because I had something to say to him. The man thought that I was finally caving in to the pressure and would agree to say the fictitious things that they wanted me to admit to, hence, he went happily to call his superior.

When the officer came he said to me, 'Well, how are you today?'

'You can see how I am,' I replied.

'So tell us the truth,' the man told me.

'All that I have told you *is* the truth. If you want to torture me more, it would be better to shoot me for I have no more truth to tell you.'

After thirteen sleepless nights and seven days of non-stop walking, my body and mind were in an indescribably miserable condition. It seemed to me that my mind had ceased to function. Then they consulted amongst themselves, and on the eighth day, were kind enough to allow me to lie down. When I lay down I was so far gone that I fell into a deep slumber immediately oblivious to the swarms of mosquitoes that infested the room. The next morning, feeling somewhat replenished by sleep, I woke up to the buzzing of mosquitoes. I found thousands of them sticking to my body. The intense exhaustion had helped me sleep through the bites of these innumerable bloodsuckers. I requested my jailors to give me a mosquito coil but the request was never granted. In this manner I enjoyed the hospitality of the CIA in this cell for sixteen days.

During my imprisonment, none of the party office-bearers, no lawyer, and not even my family members knew of my whereabouts. I kept requesting my jailors to let me send for money from my house so that I could arrange to get cigarettes and other articles but I was denied permission to do so. After this period was over I was sent to jail.

– III –

The third arrest was on 30 August 1987, when I voluntarily courted arrest. The police were raiding Mohajir homes. They were arresting Mohajir workers and treating them brutally. If they were unable to get hold of the men, the police would raid their houses and humiliate their families and elders and sometimes even arrest them. Therefore, on the assurance of the Commissioner of Karachi and the DC Central that the Mohajirs would no longer be harassed, their cruel treatment would be stopped, and that, when I was arrested, I'd be sent directly to jail, I offered myself for arrest. But the authorities broke their promise and, instead of sending me to prison, first sent me to Jackson Police Station, Keamari, where, once again, I was put in the lock-up. This lock-up was as bad as the others. I was not allowed a bed, denied all other facilities, and treated like a common criminal. I did not speak to the SHO about it because I was sure that he was merely carrying out orders. Since I was suffering from ill-health, the authorities could have, had they been so inclined, given me a better room.

It is noteworthy that there was something dubious about my being kept in this lock-up. There were roads along three sides of it, thus it was a very open place, but the day after I arrived there, I was intrigued to see that walls were being constructed on the right and left side. Later, my own sources informed me that a plan had been hatched to murder me in that lock-up. But my life was spared by the mercy of God invoked by the prayers of the Mohajir people.

On the third day, I was transferred to jail where I was given 'C class'. Later, on my lawyer's demand in court that I should be given 'A class', commensurate with my educational qualifications, the court ordered me to be given 'B class'. Only then was I given a bed.

However, there was no interrogation this time though different representatives from the government would visit me and offer me various *deals*. I kept rejecting all of them till the end. Again and again the government offered to release me and the rest of my people on bail but I rejected their offers and told them categorically that, until every single Mohajir was released and every case withdrawn, I would not accept release.

18

G.M. Syed

I first met G.M. Syed in December 1985 when he was admitted to Karachi's Jinnah Hospital for a leg operation. My mother had died on 5 December 1985, and, on that occasion, Syed Sahib had sent me a note of condolence from the hospital. It was, therefore, my duty not only to thank him but also to go to the hospital to enquire after his health. Consequently, I went to see him and met him for the first time in my life in late December 1985.

Strange rumours abounded after this very first meeting with G.M. Syed. Our opponents attempted to spread the propaganda that the Mohajir Movement was started at the behest of G.M. Syed. Of course this lie has no foundation as I started this movement during the Nizam-e-Mustafa Movement which was officially announced on 11 June 1978 and, as I have mentioned earlier, I did not meet G.M. Syed until 1985. It is obvious that a certain religio-political party propagated this misinformation in order to discredit me in the eyes of the Mohajirs and give the impression that the MQM and Jiye Sindh movements are affiliates. However, I am thankful to God that our movement is strong enough not to be led astray. They have observed my work during our ten-year struggle and know that I am struggling for their rights and am not one for rhetorics or idle talk or one to be intimidated. As a result, to this day, I have the support of the Mohajirs. The MQM has never had a written or any other kind of agreement with Jiye Sindh. However, as far as the rights of Sindhis are concerned, I have always unconditionally supported the struggle for the rights of all the oppressed people of Sindh and still do so. The MQM is the only party that voices the rights, not just of the Mohajirs, but also of oppressed Sindhis and has been consistently working towards ameliorating their lot. We must be broad-minded enough to appreciate that the Jiye Sindh party is working for the rights of Sindhis. The difference between our aims is that we aspire for our rights remaining within the geographical boundaries of Pakistan. At the same time, I would like to say that, by labelling the Jiye Sindh organization as being inimical to Pakistan and by accusing G.M. Syed of being a traitor, or by misrepresenting his statements, we are not helping Pakistan.

* * *

It is the duty of patriotic Pakistanis to consider why G.M. Syed is talking about Sindhu Desh? Is he not the same person who first moved the resolution for Pakistan in the Sindh Assembly and had it approved? Is he not the one who later organized the Muslim League in Sindh and worked for it? How can we completely disregard his contributions? Is this justice? We should reflect upon the fact that it was the same G.M. Syed who moved the Pakistan Resolution, who initially struggled for the triumph of the Muslim League, and who opted for Pakistan. Then why is this same man demanding a Sindhu Desh today? We should reflect on the reasons for this. I appeal to the Government of Pakistan and all the political parties of Pakistan that they should not treat G.M. Syed as they treated Sheikh Mujibur Rehman. They should, in fact, try to enquire from him: 'You were one of those who were involved in the creation of this country. What are your grievances?' And then sincerely take cognizance of the grievances. If his legitimate grievances are removed, then I am confident that he will be appeased. One of the reasons why I am confident of this is that once Syed Sahib said, 'It grieves a gardener to uproot a plant that he had himself sown.'

I was saddened when I read this statement from which it was evident that he is not happy with the present stand that he has taken. His words reveal his pain and suffering. I am certain that there are valid reasons for what he is demanding today. These reasons should be analyzed and his apprehensions eliminated rather than hanging the label of 'traitor' around his neck. The injustices that Sindh has had to bear must be redressed. After all, Sindh is a province of Pakistan and those who live in it are Pakistani citizens.

What did we gain by declaring Mujibur Rehman and the Bengalis traitors? If Mujib had been allowed to assume the position he deserved because he had received the majority votes, and if the grievances of the Bengalis had been redressed, the Pakistan that we live in today might have been the same as the one that was created by the will of God and Quaid-i-Azam Mohammad Ali Jinnah's efforts.

We should learn from the tragedy of East Pakistan. It is extremely unwise to doubt the patriotism of Sindhis without hearing out their grievances. The tyranny that was perpetrated on the Sindhis on the pretext of high-waymen and thugs and the oppression of women and young men are all without parallel. If you go beyond Karachi and travel to Larkana by road, you will feel that you are passing through a colonized land. New cantonments are being established at several points. Why?

I would say that not only in Sindh but also in the other provinces of Pakistan, we should open a dialogue with their respective leaders and try to find out the grievances of their people. Khan Abdul Ghaffar Khan is no longer alive. Khan Abdul Wali Khan should be contacted; Baloch leaders should consulted. Before labelling them as traitors, the grievances of the smaller provinces should be remedied so that this country can achieve prosperity and unity. When all citizens are provided their rights, only then can a nation be secure and unified and the country is able to gain strength.

Even in a house there can be difference of opinions and some family members might even threaten to leave their home. In such cases, the elders in the family arbitrate and listen to the grievances of the angry relatives and make an attempt to redress them. Similarly, a country is like a home. All those who live in it have an equal right over it. Pakistan does not belong to any one individual or any one nationality. It belongs to all the nationalities that live in it. All have an equal right to Pakistan's resources. I am convinced that, if all were given their rights, nobody would talk of secession, everybody would be ready to make sacrifices for Pakistan as they did in the past, and the country would become strong.

19

MQM and Other Leaders of Sindh

The 1972 language riots created a vast gulf between Sindhis and Mohajirs. The two sides began to see each other as enemies. We have tried our best to convince the Sindhis that we do not want the partition of Sindh. Once again, I want to assure our Sindhi brothers that, by demanding the rights of the Mohajirs we most certainly do not want or desire that Sindh should be partitioned. But we do want that our share should be proportionate to our population. And we also strongly demand that the due rights of our Sindhi compatriots should be granted. We owe a great obligation to the Sindhis.

At the time of Partition, when we arrived in Pakistan from India, having lost many of our dear ones and our possessions in the riots and violence that followed us all through our way to our new homeland; the warmth and enthusiasm with which the Sindhis welcomed us, their warm treatment, and their generosity towards us can never be forgotten. We are greatly indebted to the Sindhis which we will repay. So, whenever there is a mutual struggle towards the betterment of Sindh, God willing, the MQM will participate with full enthusiasm in it. Even in the past our voices have merged with theirs.

As far as the Sindhi leaders' impression of the MQM is concerned, I must say that the misconceptions that have been spread about us have created the impression in their minds that today the MQM is talking about Mohajirs as a distinct nationality, tomorrow they will be demanding a separate land or separate province. I want to state categorically that, under no circumstances, do we desire the division of Sindh. We only demand our rights living within the framework of Sindh and Pakistan. However, I am thankful that this misunderstanding has been cleared to a great extent. We have tried our best to narrow the gulf between Sindhis and Mohajirs and will continue to do so. And, if the Sindhi leaders harbour any misunderstandings about the Mohajirs, we will endeavour to clear them too through our deeds.

In this regard, I would like to state that a demand for Sindhis' rights is included, along with the demand for Mohajir rights, in the Charter of Resolutions presented by us. It was for this reason that Professor Ghulam Mustafa Shah, President of the Servants of Sindh Society, Sindhi educationists and intellectuals categorically supported the Resolutions. Through these measures, misunderstandings are gradually melting away and, as soon as we are provided with an opportunity, we will conduct a detailed discussion with the Sindhi leadership, elucidate our problems to them, and resolve any misunderstanding or confusion that they might harbour in their minds about us. We hope that the Sindhi leadership will respond favourably to our positive overtures, for that is where the welfare of Sindh lies and this is the most essential need of the times.

We know that many Sindhi leaders are studying our Charter of Resolutions and the gap that had until recently existed between Sindhis and Mohajirs has greatly diminished. The strongest evidence of this is that, after being arrested on 31 October 1986, when I was released on 24 January 1987 and I went on a tour of Sindh, it was not only the Mohajirs but also a large number of our Sindhi brothers and sisters who welcomed me. My hope is that the Sindhis and Mohajirs will together struggle for the restoration of Sindh's rights.

20

MQM's Stand on the Rights of the People

The exploitative class and those political and religio-political parties whose reputations have suffered because of the emergence of the MQM spread the propaganda that we who live in Sindh are against the Punjabis and the Pakhtuns. It is stated in our Charter of Resolutions that, whoever lives in Sindh with his family (whether a Punjabi or a Pakhtun), who earns here, and spends his money here will be regarded as an inhabitant of Sindh and will have the same rights in Sindh as a Mohajir or a Sindhi.

However, in this connection, I would like to say something to our Punjabi and Pakhtun compatriots who have made Sindh their home: Now that you live in Sindh; be a part of Sindh. Speak up as a representative of Sindh against the exploitation of this land and the injustices done to it and do not put the interests of Punjab or NWFP above the interests of Sindh.

Many people seem to harbour grudges and say that they will go to Punjab, or to the NWFP if they are Pakhtuns, and tell them this, that, and the other. Why? If you live in Sindh, why do you need to go to Punjab or NWFP to speak of your problems? If you have complaints here, meet the local people and tell them. When you live in Sindh and you have made your links here, to invite others to interfere in the affairs of this province is to belittle the authority of Sindh. I will add here that the rights that we are demanding for the Mohajirs and Sindhis; we are also demanding for the Punjabi and Pakhtun settlers in Sindh. When the Mohajirs and Sindhis are given their rights, they will get theirs too.

An indicator of our line of thinking is that, when the 'Haq Parast' councillors were victorious in Hyderabad and Karachi, the message I sent them was that they should not only serve Mohajirs but that they should also serve, without discrimination, everyone who lives in the area that elected them whether Punjabi, Pakhtun, or of any other ethnicity. Also, the councillors should redress their valid grievances just as they would in the case of a Sindhi or a Mohajir. And this impartiality we demonstrated in practice.

Yet, everything we say or do is misrepresented so that the people of NWFP and the Punjab get a negative impression of the MQM and become mistrustful of us. Yet, there is not a single example of any law-abiding Punjabi or Pakhtun being wronged in any way. Our Punjabi compatriots actually live on the same streets as us. There are so many of them living in Federal B Area, North Nazimabad, North Karachi, Liaquatabad, and Gulbahar. Can anybody say that a single house belonging to any individual living there was set ablaze? Or that any of them was forced to leave his home and go away? As a matter of fact, I have told my colleagues repeatedly that they should protect the Punjabis and the Pakhtuns living in their areas and make sure that no harm comes to them even though certain communities of ours were repeatedly attacked by the drug mafia who set Mohajir houses on fire and opened fire on them.

We have made it clear that we have no quarrel with our Punjabi or Pakhtun brothers. Our struggle is for the rights of Mohajirs, and against the exploitative class; our struggle is against those people who have usurped our rights and those influential people who collaborate with the drug mafia.

21

Plans for Expansion of the MQM

Apart from Karachi and Hyderabad, the MQM is strong in Mirpurkhas, Larkana, Sukkur, in short, in virtually every town and city of Sindh. Since this question may come up: why then was the MQM not as successful in the municipal bodies elections held in urban areas as it was in Karachi and Hyderabad? In answer, I would like to point out that the seats won by us in Kotri were almost equal to those of the winning side. We also won seats in Larkana, Khairpur, Mirpurkhas, and even Thatta. However, the level of success in these places was not as high as in Karachi and Hyderabad. The reason for this was that, everywhere in Sindh, the local management of the MQM, along with the workers, had been arrested by 26 August. In addition, all the core office-bearers as well as the principal workers were either under arrest or in hiding. This meant that, in the interior of Sindh, there was no experienced MQM office-bearer or worker available for planning campaigns or selecting candidates. That was the reason why the MQM was not able to participate properly in the interior in the local bodies elections. Yet, despite this handicap, apart from Karachi and Hyderabad, the MQM was able to win in several other urban areas of Sindh.

Very often we are asked how we plan to make the MQM a part of national politics. In this context I would say, as I have said many times before, that the MQM should not be seen as an exclusively Mohajir party. Rather, the most significant feature about the MQM is the class to which its leaders and supporters belong. They all come from the oppressed and exploited class. The people of the three other provinces of Pakistan say that this class is present in their provinces as well. (I acknowledge that there is a small exploitative class among the Mohajirs as well.)

Through this movement the MQM has demonstrated to all of Pakistan that, if the exploited class wants, through sincerity and determination, it can create a powerful organization to achieve its rights. I say this to the oppressed classes of Balochistan, Punjab, and NWFP as well:

> If you feel that you are being deprived of your rights, you should create an organization like the MQM. The MQM is an example and a lesson for all the oppressed people of Pakistan. No *wadera*, landowner, or wealthy capitalist leads, runs, or supports our organization. It is the people of this very class, who are beset with problems, who lead and run this organization. That is why I say that the poor of Punjab, NWFP, and Balochistan should have the courage to struggle for their rights. I will also state clearly that we, that is the MQM, are ready to join all the oppressed classes of this country in their struggle.

22

The MQM in National Politics

Thus the MQM, in the perspective it has emerged, is working for the rights of the Mohajirs. We must keep in mind that Mohajirs are a part of this nation and citizens of this country; that they have always played a significant role at the national level, and will continue to offer their services at that level in the future as well on the condition that they are recognized at the national level. In the past, although political and religio-political parties have used Mohajirs for their own ends whenever an important national issue came up or it was time to do something for their welfare, they were sidelined as being 'unwanted elements'. But the MQM has shown by its example that people from the middle and poor classes can form a strong organization which can represent them in the Parliament. Notice how many *waderas*, landowners, and capitalists there are in the provincial assemblies. This elitist crowd has now been joined by a people who do not possess the means to even get their posters printed. Thus we have proved with our deeds, our character, and our discipline that if the working class and the poor sincerely work towards it, they can become organized and strong.

I would like to tell the people of Pakistan that the propaganda that other political and religio-political parties have spread about us is utterly shameful. Whatever is said or written in this fictitious and poisonous propaganda has been done in an insidious manner to create a negative reaction against us among the people of Pakistan and ruin our image in their eyes. For example, in Punjab and NWFP, the impression has been created that the MQM is against the Punjabis and the Pakhtuns, and that our aim is to expel them from Sindh. Whereas in our Charter of Resolutions, our views are clearly laid out. The truth is that we have entered this arena solely to secure our rights and we acknowledge the rights of all the other people of Pakistan.

Because the MQM is a success story of the lower, middle, and poor classes, it is likely that, using it as an example, people belonging to the poor classes in NWFP, Punjab, and Balochistan might establish their own organizations and begin to demand their rights. If this happens, the 'divide and rule' policy of the *waderas*, landowners, capitalists, and the bureaucracy could fail. To avoid this situation, the MQM is being misrepresented to the other provinces.

Former Prime Minister Mohammad Khan Junejo did the right thing by inviting all the political parties and organizations of the country, without discrimination, on the basis of whether he shared their views or not, to sit at one table for consultation on an important national issue. May God make this attitude a tradition among us for, if this practice is carried on, many of our country's problems can be settled peacefully through discussion and negotiation. It was certainly a very good endeavour. However, I would like to appeal to my Sindhi, Punjabi, Pakhtun, and Baloch brothers and sisters to seriously and honestly consider the following: In a national conference to which, besides national level parties, all parties established on the basis of region, language, and sect were invited, was it fair to leave out a party that indisputably represented fifteen million of the country's population? No other party in the country had the distinction of having two of its candidates elected unopposed to the positions of Mayor and Deputy Mayor in two major cities of the country, Karachi and Hyderabad and, yet we were neglected.

It has always been said that the people of Karachi play an important role in the politics of the country. At this important event, when a significant national issue was to be discussed, it was not the MQM that was ignored; it was the people of Karachi and Hyderabad who were left out, for being 'unwanted elements', because the MQM is undisputedly the most widely supported and popular party among the people of these two cities. Wouldn't this exclusion make them and supporters of MQM in other cities of Sindh wonder why their representative party was not included in the deliberations?

To the people who ask us if, in the future, the MQM will be able to play a significant role in national politics, I say: 'Despite every attempt to sideline the MQM, this party has already begun to play its part in national politics. Is to become a model for the oppressed a minor achievement? To tell them, 'Do not be dominated by landowners and *waderas* but come boldly into the arena. There are no landowners, *waderas*, or capitalists in the MQM. Neither Altaf Hussain, Azeem Ahmed Tariq, nor anybody else in our ranks, belongs to those classes. We are all poor, working class people. We educated ourselves by giving tuitions.'

It is our endeavour to teach this lesson to the poor of the entire country that, in order to bring about a change in the country or to secure one's rights, it is not necessary to look to the rich and the mighty. What is now to be seen is whether the oppressed classes, irrespective of which province they belong to, learn this lesson from the MQM or not. If they decide to do so, we are ready to work alongside them. Why is the impression that we are not capable of participation on the national level spread by certain elements? I ask those elements to name a single party that enjoys equal level of popularity among the people of all the provinces. Why is it said only about the Mohajirs that they are confined only to Sindh and cannot play a part on a national level?

Nobody can deny the fact that, in all political movements that have taken place over the past forty years, the people of Karachi and Hyderabad have played an extremely important role. Public opinion in these cities has influenced the politics of the entire country. In the last Municipal elections, such people became councillors who, on account of their poverty, could never have dreamt of rising to this office. The effects of this change will definitely spread to other parts of the country and into national politics as well. Perhaps all this will take some time but I feel certain that the deprived and oppressed of the other provinces, too, will learn from the success of the MQM and the change that it has brought in Karachi and Hyderabad.

23

MQM's Afghan Policy

The MQM sees the Afghan issue in the context of the national interest and desires a solution which is in the best interest of the country. Everybody knows that the two superpowers [United States and Soviet Union] have been in conflict over this issue for a long time. They are now nearly finished with their negotiations. It is in our national interest not to get our country involved in the conflicts of these two superpowers. Our position should be that, instead of becoming instruments in the hands of the superpowers, our own interest should be of foremost importance. Our endeavour should be to see that all the Afghans who have sought refuge here should go back once the Soviets are out of Afghanistan. We should not lay any conditions as to the form of government that Afghanistan should establish because that would be tantamount to interference in another country's internal affairs which is not in the interest of Pakistan. Moreover, interference in another country's affairs would provide an opening to other countries to begin interference in our internal affairs. Would the Pakistani people like it if India or the Soviets or the US began to decide for us what kind of government Pakistan ought to have? Obviously, they would not. In brief, if the Afghan refugees are not happy with the government in Afghanistan, they should initiate a movement of their own through demonstrations or holding elections or whatever way they think is right. Why should we allow others to use our country?

What kind of wisdom is there in constantly sacrificing our own interests for the sake of other people? In this connection, the strongest argument that is forwarded is that we should help the Afghans because of the Islamic bond of brotherhood we have with them. But if this is the case, then which borders have we opened up for the Muslims of India who frequently become target to violence? Can we open up our frontiers and allow them to come here? We obviously cannot do that nor would India like that. Our rulers and political parties should keep the interest of the country and its people above all expediency. In our own country, thousands of people are affected by starvation and poverty. Consider the condition of Thar in Sindh. Similarly, countless villages in NWFP, Balochistan, and Punjab are suffering from intense poverty. Islam teaches that charity must begin at home. Hence, we should solve the problems of our own country-men first—they are both Muslims as well as Pakistanis. If we can welcome Afghans on the basis of the Islamic bond of brotherhood, the question that comes to one's mind is:

What have those poor Pakistanis done who have been languishing in dire straits in the Red Cross camps of Bangladesh for seventeen years beset by poverty and helplessness? Was it a crime that they helped the Pakistan Army in keeping aloft the flag of Pakistan in the face of an attacking enemy and a hostile environment? Why have those Muslim Pakistanis not been brought to Pakistan on the basis of Islamic brotherhood?

All kinds of justifications are given for ignoring their pleas and, apart from the injustice being meted out to them through refusing them to be repatriated here, we are injuring the trust of patriotic Pakistanis here.

What I would like to know is that, when it is a question of the Pakistanis stuck in Bangladesh, why do our political parties, especially the religio-political parties, forget all about Islamic brotherhood? The people languishing there have rendered sacrifices for Pakistan not just once but twice in their lifetime. They first [in 1947] forfeited their homes, their young sons, their honour, and their possessions to migrate to what was then East Bengal and, the second time, [in 1971] they expended their energies in defending the unity of Pakistan during the East Pakistan debacle. But, in return, they received hunger, poverty, disease, and deprivation. As for the Islamic brotherhood, the first claimants to that are the Mohajirs of East Pakistan and I make a very strong appeal to the Government of Pakistan to repatriate them here. It is their national right. They were Pakistanis before East Pakistan became Bangladesh and, even now, they fly the Pakistani flag on their camps. If we do not help these people, we would be disregarding the tenets of Islam and we would be culpable.

The infant who was born when Bangladesh was created is a grown-up now. The girl, who was of marriageable age when the new state seceded, is entering middle-age now. Her hair shows streaks of silver but there is no one to marry her off. Her brothers and parents died for Pakistan. Is it fair that our sister remains unmarried because her family gave up their lives for Pakistan? What kind of a law is that? I get thousands of letters from them but I can do nothing except weep for them. If I am receiving such letters, wouldn't the government be receiving them too? But hats off to the authorities for their eyes remain dry and their hearts never miss a beat. Today, small children and young boys whom their parents must have aspired to educate are looking for empty tin cans and glass in the garbage dumps which they can sell so that they are able to buy food for the handicapped, the ill, and the elderly in their families. Numerous daughters, sisters, and widows languish in those camps. This is a great tragedy and we have not attempted to solve it. Are we not provoking the wrath of God on us by our callousness? Could it happen that their helpless moans prove to be calamitous for us?

The political and religio-political parties, in order to oppose the MQM, make bold claims that they firmly believe in the Pakistani nationality. I ask them, what is the nationality of the Pakistanis who lie languishing in the Red Cross camps of Bangladesh? Why don't these parties raise their voices for them? For the Afghans they have all the sympathy but not a word of empathy for them. When the political parties got a chance to have a face-to-face talk with the Prime Minister, they should have broached the subject of the Pakistanis trapped in the Bangladeshi camps along with the Afghan issue, but they did not do so.

24

The Political Predictions of Pir Sahib Pagara

Being a citizen of this country, Pir Sahib has the right to air every thought that crosses his mind. Every citizen has the right to express his opinion. Earlier, Pir Sahib had made the prediction that whoever wins in the elections (Local Bodies, November 1987) would be from the Muslim League. Time proved that this did not happen. Subsequently, with more tenacity then veracity, Pir Sahib predicted that the MQM Councillors will join the Muslim League. Indeed, if the Muslim League presents a model of hands-on hard work for the oppressed classes, not only the MQM but also the whole country will join the Muslim League. But, at this point, the Mohajirs are not prepared to trust mere words because they have been doing so for forty years to no avail. Therefore, after their victory, the Haq Parasts remained Haq Parasts and did not approach the Muslim League and, in future too, God willing, the MQM people will stay united and steadfast under the standard of the MQM. However, I repeat that Pir Sahib has every right to his views.

In connection with Pir Sahib's declaration, I would like to say that we are ready to collaborate with not just the Muslim League but with any political and religio-political parties (whether PPP, Jamaat-e-Islami, Jamiat-e-Ulama-e-Pakistan, NDP or ANP), that acknowledges and respects the rights of the Mohajirs and recognizes their status because our goal is to solve problems and not to be embroiled in rivalries. We have no personal enmity towards anybody nor do we hold a grudges against anyone. We have always declared this clearly.

25

The Local Police Force in Sindh

It is often said that the people of Karachi do not like to join the police force at the lower level. However, I can confidently say that, if the recruitment process was straightforward and transparent, local people would have joined it in large numbers. I demand that the recruitment rules of the police force be made more just. For example, the people of Sindh usually have a somewhat smaller physique from that of Punjabis and Pakhtuns. Therefore, to make the Pakhtun or Punjabi physique the standard for recruitment is unfair and smacks of being ill-intentioned. It can be interpreted as a deliberate attempt to keep most of the people of Sindh from acquiring jobs in the police. What is more egregious about this is that the Sindh police does not have its own rules and the rules under which recruitment is conducted, and the whole institution run, comes under the 'Punjab Police Act'! Is this not injustice to the people of Sindh? It is obvious that the rules need to be changed. The government should empower us to manage the recruitment of police constables for just one month. If we are not able to recruit more people from Sindh, then the government can claim to be right in its complaint about them preferring not to join the police force.

If the height of a local inhabitant is less than 5 feet 6 inches, it does not mean that his performance would necessarily be inferior to that of someone who is of the specified height. Similar things used to be said about the people of Bengal: that they were weak; their physique was too slight; they were too short and, therefore, they were ineligible for military service. But when these same short and emaciated Bengalis joined the Mukti Bahini, the performance they displayed was . . . well, I'd rather not comment on it.

Geographical and climatic variations of different regions have an impact on the physique and stature of the populace of that region. Therefore, the rules of recruitment in each region should be in keeping with these geographical and climatic impacts on their inhabitants. However, not all boys in Sindh are short and some do meet the requirements. But the treatment they receive during the training period is such that they are forced to leave their jobs. They are harassed in all kinds of ways and subjected to what is clearly discriminatory treatment. Recently, there was an incident in Karachi in which hundreds of trainees ran away from the Baldia Town Police Training Camp as a consequence of the cruel and unjust treatment they received. They could not bear the abusive language and the brutal handling that was meted out to them.

For how long can such injustices be tolerated? It is our view that training camps should have local trainers because such abrasive and crass behaviour is not a part of our culture and, when our boys are exposed to it, they become upset. In addition, the boys are deliberately treated in a discriminatory manner and thus they have no option but to abscond. The police are supposed to be gracious and polite and this applies particularly to trainers.

There is a long list of suggestions enumerated at the end of the book on how to control the law and order situation in Karachi. But, as mentioned above, the most important need in this regard is that, from its highest echelons to its lowest rung, the police force should be comprised of local people. I am certain that, if the chief of Karachi police and others in the force had been natives of Karachi, they would not have allowed the victimization of innocent citizens in different parts of the city as happened on several tragic occasions recently. If the police force is made up of locals, it would also be more effective administratively. A pertinent analogy here is of a household. If it is run by a member of the household who is familiar with the problems and temperaments of its inhabitants, he will be better equipped to run it smoothly rather than someone who is an outsider. In a nutshell, it is imperative for the police force to comprise of locals—this must be recognized and implemented as soon as possible.

26

The Quota System in Sindh and MQM's Stand on the Population of Karachi

It has been our demand from the very first day that, instead of the unjust quota system, a system should be introduced whereby the Mohajirs and the Sindhis are given their share in all spheres proportionate to their population: be it in employment, admission to educational institutions, in every aspect of life at both provincial and national levels. However, the bias against them is evident not only in employment opportunities and admissions to educational institutions but also in all aspects of life. Why, I would like to know, was Hanif Khan retired from national hockey? Was he too old or too weak to be retained? Whether it is the hockey team or the cricket team, nepotism is present everywhere. An end should be put to this unfair practice. Sindh should have a quota in sports also which should be further split according to the ratio of its Sindhi and Mohajir populations.

The population of Karachi is in no way less than ten million; perhaps it is even more than that. Another fact is that its population is growing faster than that of any other city in Pakistan. That is why it is essential that the government should conduct a census here which should be reliable and done on a priority basis. Once the results of the census are known, all work in Karachi must be carried out on the basis of its population.

27

Mohajirs: A Separate Nationality

After the birth of Pakistan, five different nationalities represented their land and their culture in the new country. In 1971, the Bengalis became a nation in their own right. From then to now, four nationalities in this country have enjoyed a bona fide and recognized position while one large cultural, historical, and linguistic group, popularly known as Mohajirs, has been completely deprived of any kind of collective or legal identity. In this context, it is tragic that many individuals in this very group do not recognize this unpleasant fact as a consequence of which this ethnic group is the victim of political hatred and economic angst. Moreover, this group of Mohajirs has never attempted to get recognized as a nationality. When the MQM tried to infuse the desire of the Mohajir public with the desire for identity, they were branded as being 'biased' and 'enemies of the country'. On the other hand, the other nationalities in Pakistan do everything to secure their political and economic future. The basic reason for this is that these nationalities are deeply conscious and confident of their 'nationality', and they have never needed to convince anybody about it. They know who they are and what they want. On the contrary, the Mohajirs kept refusing to acknowledge that they are a nationality and they never tried to recognize or have others recognize their identity. In consequence, they have been degraded to such a level of humiliation and indignity that, if they are not rescued from it, the situation might end in another national tragedy.

How can Mohajirs be considered a 'nationality' in Pakistan? To prove that they are, it is necessary to study what is a 'nationality' in a historical perspective so that Mohajirs can defend their claim to being a 'nationality' with evidence and self-assurance.

The words 'nation', 'nationality', 'group' or 'tribe' have consistently been used from ancient to the present times. However, if we go back to the beginning and try to examine what comprised a 'nationality', we will find that 'nationality' had different meanings at different periods of history. These conceptual changes of 'nationality' may be divided into three periods.

I. The Tribal Period

The period in which people were recognized on the basis of their tribe was known as the tribal period. In this period, nationalities were often identified by their prophets. In the hunter-gatherer stage, the word 'nationality' was commonly used to denote tribes. The means of communication were limited and people were confined to their own small areas. The head of the tribe was responsible for tribal or inter-tribal matters. The tribes were known by the names of their chiefs or tribal elders. In this modern age, too, some residue of the tribal age can be seen in various districts of NWFP and Balochistan where the influence of the chiefs is greater than the writ of the government.

On the basis of conflicting interests or harmonious relations of different tribes, alliances began to develop between tribes which consequently resulted in the evolution of having a supreme 'Head' over the other heads of the various tribes forming the alliance. As these 'Heads' became more powerful, they evolved into *rajas*, kings, and emperors. And all those who came under the circle of their dominance were known as a 'nation'. About the same time, when the age of religions commenced and the prophets began to appear, different tribes began to be merged as 'nations' by the common religion that they shared. Their names were often linked to the names of their prophet.

There is clear evidence in the Holy Quran of these evolving concepts of nationhood or nationality. For example:[1]

> Said the chiefs of Pharaoh's
> People: 'Will you leave
> Moses and his people. . . .' (7:127)

> Said Moses to his people:
> 'Pray for help from Allah,
> And (wait) in patience and
> constancy. . . .' (7:128)

Here the concept of nationhood is clearly linked to the prophets. Once again in *Surah Al-Arāf*:

... And Moses
Had charged his brother Aaron
(Before he went up):
'Act for me amongst my people:
Do right, and follow not
The way of those
Who do mischief.' (7:142)

And Moses chose seventy
Of his people.... (7:155)

From these quotations from the Holy Quran, two of the concepts about nations or nationalities are corroborated: One, Pharaoh's nation, i.e. a nation known by the head of the tribal heads, or king. Second, Moses' nation, i.e. a nation known by its prophet or its religion.

These references seem to point to an age when different tribes or groups were being amalgamated in the larger domains of a single kingdom or followers of a single religion. What is noteworthy here is that, the smaller units—tribes or groups—that entered these larger domains, continued to retain their identity. Not only was an existing identity maintained but, for the sake of administrative efficiency, it was not considered subversive for new groups within the larger domain to retain their own identity to the extent that God not only approved of the existence of the smaller groups or sects within His preferred nation, He even divided it into smaller groups or sects.

God says in *Surah Al-Arāf*:

> Of the people of Moses
> There is a section
> Who guide and do justice
> In the light of truth. (7:159)

> We divided them into twelve Tribes
> Or nations. . . .
> When his (thirsty) people asked
> Him for water: 'Strike the rock
> With your staff': out of it
> There gushed forth twelve springs:
> Each group knew its own place
> For water. (7:160)

Similarly, in *Surah Al-Hujurāt*:

> O mankind! We created
> You from a single (pair)
> Of a male and a female,
> And made you into
> Nations and tribes, that
> You may know each other
> (Not that you may despise
> Each other). (49:13)

It is clear from the words of God that sects, tribes, nations, and nationalities fulfil the purpose of identity, national or individual, and exist not only in accordance with the Divine Will but are also sanctioned by God. To reject this, or to refuse to acknowledge an individual's or group's identity, is either based on ignorance or injustice.

Earlier, however, the nomadic tribal society that had depended on hunting, foraging for fruit, etc., for its sustenance went through various stages of evolution to arrive at the feudal structure of agricultural societies. This age may be called the second age or the feudal age.

II. The Feudal Age

A new social order brings changes not only to the mode of life and the common demands of the old social order but also to its thinking. Therefore, we find that, in the feudal age, the concepts of the nomadic age about nations and nationalities also underwent a change. When large land ownerships combine, states and *rajwaras* (principalities) come into being and, from them, kingdoms and empires take form. It is from here that the concept of nationality linked to state, region, or country evolved. Besides being linked to the head of a tribe, king, religion, and prophet—nations or nationalities began to be known also by the names of the region, state, or country to which they belonged. Here it is important to note that even now the tribal and feudal systems are influential factors in the provinces of Pakistan.

III. The Modern Age

A state or a country, especially a federal state, is an amalgamation of units. Each unit or nationality is built on the basis of a shared culture, mode of life, and language and they all remain united as one nation as long as their economic interests are not hurt. But, if their economic interests are threatened because of their cultural or linguistic divergence, the unity of the nation begins to rupture and new units and nationalities emerge.

In the present era, the definitions of nation and nationality are the products of the modern industrial age which came after the tribal, agricultural, and feudal ages. Although the origin of the concept of nationhood in the modern industrial age may be traced back to Poland, it was the French Revolution of the eighteenth century that put forward the momentous concept of freedom namely, Liberty, Fraternity, and Equality. This new concept spelt the end of monarchy. With the advent of the French Revolution, the aristocratic feudal system in France breathed its last. After France, this new concept spread to all of Europe opening new paths to progress. It was around the time that the French Revolution took place that the Industrial Revolution gained impetus in England. With the rise of guilds, industry, and trading, a middle class gained ascendency and the hold of the feudal age gave way to the industrial age. Hitherto the Pope and the Church had enjoyed a high political status and influence but, with the advent of the industrial age, their elevated status was snatched away from them. As soon as Europe stepped into the modern industrial age, it discarded religion as the foundation of nationality and European countries began to look for opportunities all over the world to create a market for their industrial produce; hence, colonies began to emerge.

The sea routes had been opened up earlier. In the fifteenth century the Portuguese explorer, Vasco de Gama, sailed past the Cape of Good Hope on the southernmost region of Africa and founded the route to India and the Far East. In the sixteenth century, Albuquerque landed in South India and founded Goa. Cooke discovered Australia and New Zealand in the eighteenth century. Briefly, it was an age of searching for places to set up new colonies, new sources of economic wealth, and new markets. This age is known as the Age of Enlightenment. The philosopher, Jean Jacques Rousseau, whose political theories helped bring about the French Revolution, defined his 'Social Contract Theory' which forms the basis of political science. In England, John Stuart Mill came up with the concept of 'democracy' and earlier Adam Smith wrote his *Wealth of Nations* which is the first economic treatise.

Note

1. The translations of the *Surahs* are from Abdullah Yusuf Ali's English translation of the Holy Quran.

28

Nation and Nationality

After this discourse, the difference between a 'nation' and a 'nationality' should be comprehensible. To put it concisely, a 'nation' was first identified by its tribal head, prophet, or religion. Later the concept of 'nation' became more strongly linked to a state. It was on this basis that the League of Nations was formed to resolve the issues arising between nations. It was followed by the United Nations. In the United Nations, state and nation are synonymous concepts and nations are linked to geographical boundaries and the state. It is noteworthy that, at first, the United Nations comprised only a few members. Between the period of the United Nations' coming into being and now, numerous new states and nations have joined the organization after breaking away from older states and nations. The number of its member countries has now increased to 153.

Some of the countries and nations, after they ceased to be colonies, were splintered into new countries and nations though remaining within the same geographical boundaries as before. These facts prove that a nation can give birth to more nations within the same geographical area. Essentially, in the present era, a nation is a body of population that lives within a particular geographic or political unit. They are recognized by the name of their states, for example, the Indian, Pakistani, Saudi, Yemeni, Indonesian, Chinese, etc. nations.

A nation can possess different nationalities. Some countries are geographically vast and comprise of people belonging to different cultures and languages. Their psychological responses are also different. Therefore, even though they may live within the geographical confines of a single state as nationalities, they may still maintain their particular identity. A country (state) is not necessarily one homogeneous entity; rather it is usually a mixture of varied elements. When this assortment of different elements (of linguistic and cultural groups) is confined within a single unit, it is known as a nation.

The concept of Pakistan and the Two-Nation Theory developed many years prior to Partition. Sir Syed Ahmed Khan laid the foundation of this theory. It is therefore historically justified to proclaim that Sir Syed was the architect of the Two-Nation Theory. However, one has to remember that the two-nation concept of today is different from Sir Syed Ahmed's because he had envisaged all the Muslims of the subcontinent as one nation and all the Hindus as another. But what we have done today is that we have recognized the people of the majority Muslim provinces as one nation while excluding the Muslims of the Muslim minority provinces from being a part of the Muslim nationhood. Before Sir Syed put forward the Two-Nation Theory, the Indian populace never regarded religion as a differentiating factor. But Sir Syed's far-sightedness made him realize that the Hindus' political efforts were completely energized towards achieving goals which were solely in their own interest and they also enjoyed the blessings of the British while the Muslims had failed in bringing any sense of order in their own political ranks. Hence, he came upon the realization that the Muslims and Hindus of the sub-continent were two separate nations. This was elucidated by him in his magazine, *Tehzeeb-ul-Iqhlaque*, and his public addresses. Afterwards, when the Indian National Congress was founded in 1885, he appealed to the Muslims not to join it because the Hindus and Muslims were two separate nations.

From 1857 to 1904, Sir Syed Ahmed's Two-Nation Theory increased the sense of awareness amongst the Muslims of their separate identity. Subsequently, in 1906, Nawab Viqar-ul-Mulk, Mohsin-ul-Mulk, and Sir Aga Khan prepared a petition which they presented to the British government in which they demanded that the rights of Muslims in India be protected. It is interesting to note that, at that stage, the demand was not for a separate homeland but for the protection of the rights and economic future of the Muslims. Sir Syed Ahmed's Two-Nation Theory had wrought a revolution in Muslim thinking. It had now become incumbent upon them to bring a sense of order into their political ranks. In order to achieve this, Sir Aga Khan, Nawab Viqar-ul-Mulk, Nawab Mohsin-ul-Mulk, and Nawab Salimullah Khan laid the foundation of the All-India Muslim League in Dacca (now Dhaka) in 1906. Thus, the creation of both the Congress and the Muslim League meant that both the Hindus and the Muslims began to consolidate themselves as separate nations within the geographical boundaries of one country—India. By 1940, the Muslims of India put forward their demand for Pakistan on the basis of their being a separate nation. Inherent in their demand was the Muslim nation's link with a homeland and their belief in a separate identity. Here it is necessary to remember that the Two-Nation Theory was the genesis of Muslim nationhood in the subcontinent and when the idea of a distinct Muslim nationhood strengthened, it developed into the demand for a separate nation. On 14 August 1947, the new state of Pakistan emerged on the map of the world and the new Pakistani nation became a member of the United Nations. Hence, it was through such a process that one country was born from another and one nation from another.

29

The Beginnings of the Mohajir Nationality

The Mohajir nationality had its beginnings in the Two-Nation Theory. Pakistan is a member of the United Nations and in it a nation is known by its country and a nation is that in which different nationalities come together. A nation is bound to comprise different nationalities. Take Pakistan, for example. It comprises of Bengalis (no longer), Pakhtuns, Sindhis, Punjabis, and the Baloch which are distinct nationalities. Thus Pakistan is one nation and one state but there are several nationalities residing in it.

After a few years of the establishment of Pakistan, the Bengalis began to become restless. They felt that their interests, their progress, and their future were at risk. It was this sense of insecurity that gave rise to Bengali nationalism. One must not forget that these were the same Bengalis who had voted for Pakistan. From 1947 to 1971, Bengal was not a nation but simply a nationality. But when the Bengalis began to feel that their economic interests were at stake; their path to progress blocked; and their security uncertain, the desire for a separate nation began to develop. It eventually grew into Bengali nationality that aspired to become a separate nation or state. And, in 1971, with the creation of Bangladesh, the Bengalis came to be recognized as a separate nation and was accepted as such by the United Nations.

India had, initially, given birth to two states causing the two large subordinate nationalities of the nation to become two separate nations. What this means is that, first a nationality takes shape, which, under certain conditions, can become a nation.

Before 1971, Pakistan was accepted by the United Nations as a single entity. Its political and geographic boundaries were acknowledged and respected but, when the Bengali nationality insisted on independence and took their struggle to the extreme of breaking away, the world had no choice but to acknowledge and afford recognition to their new country, Bangladesh. Hence, the region that had separated itself from India and had become Pakistan was further split into two separate countries. The reason being a sense of deprivation born out of a loss of hope about being afforded security and progress in the existing set-up; and a sense of awareness of being a nationality followed by an intensification of that awareness. This is the process through which nationalities evolve into nations.

History repeatedly teaches us that, if the rights of a certain population of a federation are crushed with the use of force or that, rather than providing them with equal rights, attempts are made to subjugate them, the result is similar to what happened in our eastern wing. An army of 93,000 soldiers became prisoners of war (POWs); the blood of a million people was shed; and a nationality became a nation.

Yuri Gankovsky, a renowned professor, writing in his book, *Peoples of Pakistan,* has mentioned the different nationalities of Pakistan. But there is no reference to the Mohajir nationality. Yet, it is clear that there are, undeniably, four different major nationalities residing in Pakistan currently.

30

The Desire to Maintain the Identity of a Nationality

The presence of independent states, regions, provinces, or countries emerging from all the theories of nationhood and nationalities in the past and present is fundamentally the outcome of a need in society. Society, in turn, consists of individuals. Now the question arises, why do people organize themselves into tribes, regions, provinces, states, and countries and why do they become part of a society? The answer to this is that they do so for a better present and future for themselves; for the survival of their future generations; and to live their lives in accordance with their own desires. In other words, a country and a nation come into being for political, economic, and cultural security and the development of all those who come within its ambit. The components of a country come into being in recognition of this need—the components comprising provinces, states, and nationalities.

If all the people living in a country are provided equal opportunities to secure and further their political, linguistic, economic, and cultural goals, then the concept of different nationalities in that country grows weaker and the ideal of a united nation becomes stronger. If, on the other hand, equal opportunities are not available to all the nationalities, then the concept of a separate nationality in that country grows stronger and the concept of a united nation grows weaker.

In other words, if the components of a united nation are deprived of equal opportunities or development and the security of their interests; if, instead of a sense of equality and fraternity, there develops the feeling of being subjugated by other nationalities or of being oppressed, then that united nation provides a reason for nationalities living within its ambit to become more conscious of themselves as a separate entity. A nationality's struggle in the beginning is to ensure that their rights and security are granted. If the response to this demand is realistic, tolerant, and wise the fulfilled nationality will settle down as a productive component of the united nation. But if its voice is suppressed and its demands and movement are labelled as treachery or a foreign conspiracy and crushed, then its stance changes. Both the Pakistan and Bangladesh movements are proofs of the historical convergence of such circumstances.

The concept of a Mohajir nationality is developing under this same historical convergence. No group or class of Pakistanis can deny that the Mohajirs are an exceptionally dynamic component of this nation. They offered the most sacrifices in bringing Pakistan into existence. The contribution of the Mohajirs in steadying and supporting Pakistan in its earliest days is the highest of any section or nation. They played a dominant role in the industrial and economic progress of the country. They have always been in the vanguard of political and professional movements and organizations. In science and literature, journalism and broadcasting, fine arts and architecture; in fact, there are few areas in which Mohajirs have not played a fundamental role. But what has been their reward?—the 2 per cent quota; domicile; discrimination between the rural and the urban; and the status of a second-class citizenry.

The result is that their future is dark. Their earlier generation lies buried in Pakistan's soil; the second generation is in the twilight of their lives, and their third generation has grown up; yet they are not considered sons of the soil. They have no place in the highest echelon of power, their right to employment is small, and their admission to technical schools limited. If such are the prospects of the present generation, what will become of the next generation? Under such conditions the awareness of nationality is bound to emerge. There will be the struggle for rights; a strife to secure pledges for the future. How can it be otherwise?

Are there any more doubts about the emergence of a common nationality among people whose circumstance and interests are the same; who have the same beginning and the same perceived end; and the same traditions and culture? But some people still stubbornly and consistently reject the fact that the Mohajirs comprise a nationality.

As I have said before, the tribal or feudal systems are still effectively extant in some of the provinces of Pakistan. On the other hand, neither the ancient tribal system nor the archaic feudal system is in force among the Mohajirs. They are associated with the modern industrial and technological age. Therefore, to force the Mohajir nationality to renounce the modern concept of nationality and be absorbed in the outmoded age of feudalism is to attempt to turn the wheels of history backwards which is bound to fail.

In the same way the Mohajir culture and civilization are also in harmony with the demands of the modern age. We can give a classic example of this in the language of Urdu which is the mother tongue of a majority of the Mohajirs. Although, from a historical perspective, Urdu is not a very old language, it is a fact that Urdu is the mode of expression of the largest number of thinkers, scientists, writers, journalists, poets, and historians in Pakistan. It is the treasure trove of knowledge on all subjects related to life and culture and has contributed to the value system of our society. In contrast, the other languages spoken in Pakistan, although historically and culturally thousands of years old and rich in their own right, have still not been successful in assimilating modernity. That is why, despite being a relatively new language, Urdu has the largest store of information and literature of all the languages of Pakistan.

Another important aspect is that Urdu has the largest quantity of translated foreign literature. This is only because it is able to meet the demands of the modern age. The competence of this language lies in that it can be used as a medium to write on any subject.

In conclusion, the question I wish to put is this: Since Mohajirs are not Pakhtun, Sindhi, Punjabi, or Baloch—what are they? It is common knowledge that other nationalities of Pakistan know us as Mohajirs and call us Mohajirs. We have our own distinct language, culture, interests, and style of living which is different from the others and which give us a separate and clear identity.

The Mohajir caravans that arrived in Pakistan in 1947 brought with them a cultural revolution and an intellectual awakening. With the act of migration, what accompanied the Mohajirs into Pakistan was the unparalleled culture of the subcontinent, valuable traditions, incomparable history, and the precious treasures of a shared Urdu language.

In common usage, the meaning of *hijrat* is 'emigration from one's homeland'. But the Muslim migration from the Muslim minority provinces of India to Pakistan has a special significance because it was not the act of a few individuals but of a very large group of people whose culture was not of any particular region but was the expression of a shared spiritual life, common fine arts, mode of thinking, and the result of a deep intellectual unity and social intermixing. The renowned intellectual and historian Pir Syed Hisamuddin Shah has illustrated this phenomenon in the following words:

> *When there was exodus from India (in 1947) only then Karachi was populated.'* (*Quami Zubaan*, December 1982).

31

The Reasons for MQM's Popularity

There are two reasons why organizations created in the name of the Mohajirs, in the days before the MQM, could not gain popularity. One reason is that the organizations existed only on paper. The other reason is that they were controlled by people behind the scenes while their ostensible office-bearers were a different set of people. On the contrary, the MQM is controlled by the people who run it—its office-bearers and its workers. We proudly claim that, not only in the history of Pakistan but in the history of the whole subcontinent, no similar organization exists.

What normally happens in other parties is that there is much talk of the poor but those who resort to such rhetoric are people who have never for a moment experienced poverty. How can they know what the anxieties and problems of the poor are? How can they be aware of what the poor go through to educate their children or to buy new clothes for them at Eid? What do they know about the travails of travelling in public transport? What do they know about the difficulties faced by poor households as they fail to stretch their meagre incomes to the end of each month?

The MQM is the first organization of its kind in Pakistan which was not only created by poor people but is also run by the underprivileged and that is the main reason for our success. While other organizations kept looking all over for support, we relied entirely upon ourselves. Other reasons for our success are that we work with scrupulous honesty and in a scientific manner. Moreover, we are blessed with extremely sincere, selfless, and honest workers whose tireless efforts have assisted us in bringing the MQM where it stands today. Instead of accepting the patronage of anyone, I handed the guardianship of MQM to my colleagues. This organization is being run by Mohajir workers themselves who make all decisions.

32

Enmity with the MQM

For a long time, the bureaucracy and the enemies of the MQM have practised certain tactics to ensure that the MQM remains disturbed and unable to relax and plan its future strategy. After my release from prison, I adopted an extremely positive and conciliatory attitude in my public statements and speeches. While addressing the Karachi Press Club's programme, 'Meet the Press', I went to the extent of apologizing to anyone who, in the course of the last ten years, had in any way been hurt by any remark that I might have made in my speeches or writings. But those forces which do not want Mohajirs to unite on a single platform did not respond positively to my appeals and overtures of goodwill. Instead, they carried on with their propaganda and maintained their hostile attitude.

After the victory of 'Haq Parast' councillors in Karachi and Hyderabad, the petty and vicious tactics our opponents used to discredit our tenure are without parallel. Gutter lines in the city were artificially blocked. Polythene bags filled with gravel and bricks were deliberately thrown into gutters to make them overflow. Sanitary workers were bribed to go on strike. They were encouraged to make trouble for MQM members and workers so that the people would hold the party responsible for the deteriorating civic environment all over the city. Garbage was dumped on the city's roads. They resorted to such tactics but, fortunately, the Mohajir public realized that it was all a ploy to ensure the failure of MQM. As for the sanitary workers' strike, when that took place, our councillors and MQM workers swept the streets themselves and used their hands to do the cleaning. Why do the public continue to support us? Because, in the last forty years, no councillors were ever seen to sweep the roads or clean the gutters with their own hands.

Actually, all these actions against us were part of a deep and planned conspiracy to undermine the MQM so that, in future, the public may not support us. Authority was snatched from the mayor and deputy mayor. Councillors could not even verify forms for identity card or applications for passports. Furthermore, various parties started issuing pamphlets which demanded to know why people were not being given jobs now that MQM councillors have been elected? Why were the problems of the police and other problems of the city not being solved? The aim of this propaganda was to turn the masses against the MQM. The jurisdiction of the municipal bodies was to begin with limited authority but, whatever little authority they possessed had now been taken away from them.

But I am grateful to God that the Mohajir public has recognized the conspiracy. They are able to differentiate between friends and foes and have learned the extent of power the local bodies can wield and the difficulties and problems the MQM is confronting at present.

I am certain that my brothers, elders, mothers, and sisters will not be discouraged by these circumstances and the Mohajir public will confront and overcome the obstacles placed in the way of MQM with the same enthusiasm and love which they displayed on the occasion of the local bodies elections.

In the context of the persistent violence and disturbances in Karachi, I would like to say clearly that they are abetted by the drug mafia. Parties who are enemies of the Mohajirs are also involved in all such incidents. Members of the drug mafia are hired to instigate these disturbances which are later given the colour of Mohajir-Pakhtun clashes.

None of these parties took up the challenge of putting an end to violence previously but, today, they are raising a hue and cry and preaching brotherly love. Have they not heard of the bloodshed in Aligarh Colony and Qasba Colony and how infants were thrown into the fire; how unarmed people were shot dead in Shah Faisal Colony, Liaquatabad, and Nazimabad, and their houses destroyed; how our young men were killed and wounded in Sohrab Goth and Hyderabad? Newspapers have published detailed reports of all these acts of violence. Evidence exists that, when Aligarh and Qasba colonies were attacked, instructions and guidance for the assailants were being given through loudspeakers in the mosques.

The fact is that the MQM took the responsibility of running the municipal system in a difficult situation. And, as soon as it assumed office, its path was strewn with difficulties by hostile elements resorting to utterly contemptible means. But, with God's grace, I am hopeful that our Mohajir brothers will take into account the prevailing conditions. I am unhappy and distressed at their anxieties and difficulties and I am deeply grieved that very many of my Mohajir brothers have been thrown out of their homes in Shah Faisal Colony and Green Town. This causes me great anguish and we are struggling in every possible way to restore their homes to them.

But the MQM is a poor party. If the MQM was in possession of funds and land, I would, in all honesty, rehabilitate all those victimized families and compensate them for their losses. How I wish I could do that! I appeal to God, the most Exalted, Who sees all with this prayer:

See what efforts are being made to ensure that we fail. Oh Cherisher and Provider of the world, see what conspiracies are being hatched against us. You who decide what is true and what is false, I am in Your Presence now and pray to You: help us, and destroy those cruel forces who, intoxicated with their own power, are working against us; who want to see us fail; to lose our good name; who want to disgrace us. Come to the aid of our helpless families and give our Mohajir brothers the courage never to despair and never be disheartened with the MQM.

I would like to say to my Mohajir brothers, elders, mothers, and sisters that, in the struggle for rights in any movement, not only must one confront such troubles and anxieties but one also needs to cross a hurdle of fire and blood as well. Those who usurp the rights of others never return them straightforwardly and with good grace. That we should lose hope, be disheartened, and give up is exactly what our enemies desire. I ask my brothers, should we despair? No, never! We must fight these circumstances. Life and death are in the hands of God. I, too, promise my brothers and sisters that, as long as I am alive, I will remain steadfast, my colleagues will remain steadfast and, God willing, we will continue to struggle for the rights of Mohajirs.

33

Attempts on My Life

Several times my enemies have attempted to kill me. However, it is the faith of every Muslim that death comes at a time preordained by God. Unless that moment has arrived, no one can kill anyone. The fact is that there have been so many attempts on my life that I have forgotten their details. However, I will describe some of them here:

When I was a student at the University of Karachi, where I initiated the Mohajir movement, I came under two planned attacks on my life. I have briefly mentioned earlier the armed attack made on me and the workers of APMSO at the University of Karachi in February 1981. What happened on that occasion was that, on 1 February 1981, the organization's admissions campaign began. Our organization had planned our campaign a month earlier and, in order that they might demonstrate a high degree of efficiency, we had prepared our workers in a systematic manner for a full month. For the campaign, APMSO had put up five large stalls at the university. Our main stall was in front of the post office and, because of its situation and size, it was more prominent and attractive than the stalls of other students' organizations. Thus it was the cynosure of every newcomer's attention. On that day APMSO distributed admission forms to 1800 students, a record in the history of the university which is so far unbroken. This roused the rancour of the other students' organizations greatly and that very night the high command of the Jamiat-e-Tulaba decided to resort to use firearms to annihilate APMSO. We got a preliminary taste of their attack on 2 February when they beat up some of our hardworking and selfless workers.

Again, 3 February 1981 is a crucial day in the history of APMSO and the Mohajirs. On this day my colleagues and I were subjected to a murderous attack. Our sin was our struggle for the rights of Mohajir students. At 9.30 a.m., a procession of our rivals from Urdu Science College, Ship Owners' College, Jinnah College, and other colleges, entered the main gate of the University of Karachi shouting slogans of 'Altaf Hussain is a traitor and a fraud!'. They approached our stall and began to shout more provocative slogans. For an hour-and-a-half this group of a hundred armed men kept taunting our male and female student workers in an effort to provoke them. When one brave worker of ours, Ishrat Aziz went forward they attacked him with knives. When other workers tried to intervene they too were attacked in the same way and fell bleeding on the ground. As soon as they fell, the assailants brought out their guns and targeted me. But before they could press their triggers, the loyal and fearless female workers of APMSO made a circle around me and thwarted their attempts. When one of our colleagues, Abu Zar, tried to resist their onslaught, they fell on him with chains and sharp knives. One assailant tried to stab him in the back with a knife but Azeem Ahmed Tariq, who was then the Secretary General of APMSO, sprang forward and thrust his arm in front of him to block the knife as a result of which he suffered deep gashes on his wrist. Meanwhile, the ambulance arrived and I left for Abbasi Shaheed Hospital along with my colleagues and wounded workers.

Before this incident, I was the target of another armed attack in the university. The year was probably 1979. On 11 June 1978, one year after the formation of APMSO, when the Students' Union elections were being held, I also took part in the contest. During electioneering, I was carrying some pamphlets on my Honda 50 motorbike when the workers of a rival students' organization attacked me. I suffered some injuries but was, by God's grace, able to escape.

34

The Issue of Marriage

I am frequently asked the question why I have not married so far. Marriage is not only a *sunnah* of the Prophet (PBUH) but, it is also necessary from the moral, social, and economic point of view. All these arguments are very true but I live the life of a revolutionary in which I often don't have time to eat and sometimes I don't get to sleep for 48 hours at a stretch. When there is a crisis, some organizations or institutions impose an emergency but I live constantly in a state of emergency; so I never get the time to think that I should get married or that I want to marry. The fact is that I have subordinated all my desires and interests to my mission and, for me, the centre of all these things is solely the MQM. At this stage my marrying would undoubtedly hurt the movement because it will impinge on the time I should devote towards the achievement of my objective which is a prospect that is not acceptable to me under any circumstances.

If I am able to accomplish my mission, I will feel that a world full of happiness is all mine. To achieve a great goal one has to make great sacrifices. Sometimes one has to sacrifice one's children or one's whole life's savings while here we are talking of whether I should marry or not. Marriage is a personal matter and I have dedicated my person to my mission. All my siblings live in their own homes and I live alone in my house. My colleagues not only look after me, they also take care of all my personal needs. Running the house, seeing to my food and clothes—it is all done efficiently and well and I don't have to concern myself about anything. For this I give full credit to my colleagues.

35

My Family's Role in the Movement

My family has certainly contributed to the success of this movement in the sense that the troubles and anxieties they have had to put up with on my account could have compelled them to blame or distance themselves from me. But on the contrary, their attitude towards me has always remained positive. It was their positive attitude that provided me the courage to continue with the movement despite all my troubles.

I am therefore grateful to my brothers and sisters and to the rest of my family as well. In this context the most important role was played by my mother (May Paradise be her eternal home). It is very difficult for me to find words to describe her character and attitude. I was a student of B. Pharmacy at the university when I began my political activities there. As everybody knows, science students need to spend more time on their studies. Coupled with this was my involvement with the movement. As a result I was unable to fulfil my responsibilities as a member of the household. But my family, and especially my mother, never expressed any annoyance about this and their attitude towards me always remained positive.

After university hours, my colleagues and I used to give tuitions in order to defray the expenses of our education as well as the organization we were running. This was so time-consuming that I would come home at 3 or 4 a.m. every day. Even though my mother suffered from ill health, she would routinely wake up when I got home, open the door for me, and would enquire if I had eaten or not. I never saw her with an expression of anxiety on her face although I knew how worried she was. It is natural for any mother to want that her children do not get themselves involved in something that can bring them harm but my mother never discouraged me and never tried to dissuade me from organizing the movement. However, she would instruct me that I should act with prudence and sagacity to complete my mission. I, too, would try to make her understand that whoever undertook such a mission would also be someone's child. Besides, I would tell her that I was not striving for myself but all my people. And she would pray fervently and with great affection that God grant me success in my endeavour.

My mother helped to strengthen my resolve and courage at every step. When I was arrested on 14 August 1979 for demonstrating in support of expatriation of Pakistanis from Bangladesh, the government offered me various propositions to remit my sentence. I refused all these offers. As I mentioned before, I was sentenced to nine months of imprisonment with hard labour and five lashes, a punishment that would daunt any mother. Eid was round the corner so, playing upon a mother's weakness for her son, the government sent some faculty members of the University of Karachi along with the students' advisor to my mother. They told *Ammi* that, if she wrote an appeal for pardon, I would be released before Eid. However, my mother categorically refused to write such an appeal. She told them, 'My son is fighting for the Truth. It is up to you to release him or not; I am not going to plead for mercy.' After that they got in touch with my brothers but they too said what my mother had said. Which mother wouldn't want her son to be released from prison, but I salute her greatness for displaying such courage in the face of coercion and to take a decision that must have wrenched her heart. I pray that God grant such courage to the mothers of all my colleagues and workers.

My mother used to treat my friends and colleagues with great warmth and would convey their messages to me. She never showed any annoyance with me and never complained to me. She put up with all her problems with great fortitude and never said anything that might have disheartened me.

My mother always advised me to be sincere in my mission, to work for the collective good of the people, and never let my personal interests interfere with my work. She always prayed that God should help me to remain steadfast in my struggle. I thank God that I remained true to her advice—always. It is thanks to her prayers for me that I have remained resolute in the face of great trials and have never sold my conscience to anyone.

My brothers and sisters supported the movement not merely because I was their brother. As a matter of fact, they used to have arguments with me about it as other people would have before they joined the organization.

On 5 December 1985, when my mother died, I felt as though I had lost everything. For a long time after her death I felt as though I could never get over my bereavement. But now I am able to bear her loss because of the love and affection that thousands of mothers have bestowed on me by supporting me and helping me. When they come to see me and place their loving hands on my head, I feel as though it was my own mother doing this. It seems to me that God, who took away my one actual mother, has given me thousands of other mothers whose prayers are with me. May those prayers always stay with me and bless my organization.

36

Why the Stress on the Word 'Mohajir'?

As soon as one utters the word, 'Mohajir', the image that arises in one's mind is of the Pakistan Movement because it has now been proven that those who played the most significant role in the creation of Pakistan were the Muslims who resided in the Muslim-minority regions of the Indian subcontinent, and they were the ones who migrated to Pakistan. It would not be wrong to say that the word 'Mohajir' evokes a whole history and a particular mode of political thought and actions. Moreover, Mohajirs are the bearers of a vigorous civilization and culture. For these reasons no other epithet can better represent the Mohajirs.

In MQM's view, local inhabitants of Sindh are those who, irrespective of whether they speak Urdu, Sindhi, Balochi or any other language, live permanently in Sindh with their families; who earn here and spend their earnings here; who, when they die, are buried here; and whose interests are linked with the interests of Sindh.

Even before the establishment of the MQM, many organizations had been formed in Sindh with the word 'Mohajir' as part of their name. This is evidence of the fact that the word 'Mohajir' was used to identify a group.

Yet the majority of Mohajirs did not use this word in the sense of their distinct identity. The earlier organizations with 'Mohajir' in their names were not successful because they could not attract popular support. Nor did they present a clear plan of action for securing the rights of the Mohajirs. In contrast, the MQM has become a powerful people's force and the only representative voice of the Mohajirs on account of its ten years of struggle; unabated organizational work, clear concepts, and constructive policies. Because of its success, it has also attracted strong antagonism and these antagonists have been spreading many deliberate misinterpretations of the word 'Mohajir'.

Who are the Mohajirs?

Who are the people for whom MQM uses the word 'Mohajir'? I want to provide an unambiguous answer to this question so that any confusion and misunderstanding in people's minds in this regard may be cleared. MQM considers all those people to be Mohajirs:

- Who migrated from the Muslim minority provinces of the subcontinent to Pakistan as a result of the creation of Pakistan.
- Who are not a part of any of the older nationalities of Pakistan, i.e. Punjabi, Sindhi, Baloch, and Pakhtun.
- Who migrated from those parts of the Punjab where the language and culture were different from those

of Punjab. For example, the people who came to Sindh from East Punjab called themselves Punjabis, while others coming from East Punjab, whose language was other than Urdu or Punjabi, were known as Mohajirs.

Although Mohajirs are newcomers to Sindh, they have bound their lives with Sindh and have therefore, become a part of Sindh. Moreover, in the early days of Pakistan, the Mohajirs struggled hard and made valuable contributions in managing the administrative affairs of the government and the establishment of industry. Furthermore, the Government of Pakistan and the Muslim League High Command had invited them to come to Pakistan.

When Mohajirs, Sindhis, and the Baloch who had settled in Sindh a long time ago felt that the bureaucracy and exploitative forces had deprived them of their rights, they began to suffer from a shared feeling of deprivation. They also felt the need to end the misunderstandings that had developed between them because it was these very misunderstandings and animosities that had provided the exploitative forces with the opportunity to gain control of Sindh's land, industry, and resources.

Compared to the Sindhis, it took longer for the Mohajirs to become aware of the ongoing plunder. And, when this awareness came, the MQM was created with the purpose of ensuring that the Mohajirs are provided their due rights. But, because Sindhis and Mohajirs suffer from similar issues, the MQM struggles for the rights of

Sindhis also which is the reason why the MQM's message attracts Sindhis as well. Hence, when the MQM held large public meetings in Karachi, Hyderabad, Sukkur, and other cities of Sindh along with the Mohajirs large numbers of Sindhis also attended them. Judging by the extensive support given by the people at these meetings and other occasions, it became clear that the people of Sindh were displaying their complete confidence in the MQM. The people of Sindh, especially the Mohajirs at present feel that the solutions to their problems should be presented in the form of a Charter of Resolutions from the MQM platform.

37

The Kalabagh Dam

In running a federation, it is necessary that all the units participating in it should be given equal importance in the solving of national issues; and that no decision, no matter how important or beneficial, should be taken without taking them into confidence; for there is nothing more essential for a federation than unanimity and accord. I do not have all the figures and the technical details of the Kalabagh Dam before me but what I have perceived from the statements of different political and public leaders and from gatherings held at the public level is that, whatever the benefits of building the dam, the NWFP [now Khyber Pakhtunkhwa] province, and especially the province of Sindh, would suffer irreversible harm from it. This situation is turning into another cause of the sense of deprivation felt by the Sindhis at a time when they and the other smaller provinces are already aggrieved because no action has been taken on the agreement for the division of water between the provinces. Complaints of the people of Sindh and NWFP are gaining strength because there is no explanation of the plan for Kalabagh and there is a growing fear about the detrimental environmental effects that will occur with the building of the dam. Our clear stand on this is that, not only the experts and public representatives, but also the people of the four provinces be taken into confidence on this technical issue. Also, only those plans should be ratified which are not damaging to any of the provinces. There is nothing better than unanimity and accord for the stability of Pakistan.

Epilogue

In this context I suggest that the poor and oppressed people of Punjab, NWFP, Sindh, and Balochistan should create organizations similar to the MQM and ensure that their leadership comes from their own class. If the poor and oppressed in all the provinces of Pakistan establish such organizations, the MQM will give them all possible support and we will work with them. In this way, the poor people of Pakistan can together successfully challenge the exploitative forces that have impeded their progress. In particular, I want to reach out to the poor and oppressed people of Punjab and say to them, 'Come out and act because the responsibility for the continued existence of Pakistan rests with the people of Punjab.' Most of those in high positions and the bureaucracy are from Punjab. It is they who are the oppressors but the whole province of Punjab gets a bad name even though, in Punjab, there is a large class of people who are being exploited. That is why the people of the smaller provinces look to Punjab to start a vigorous struggle. If the poor and oppressed of Punjab produce their leadership from their own class, all the people of Pakistan will support them. If people from the poor and working class come to power, they will be in a better position to comprehend and solve the problems of the poor.

I would say, especially to the young, that today the opposition to the MQM is not because of its slogan of Mohajir nationality but because it has shown a new path to the poor and oppressed people of Pakistan and demonstrated that, if they want, they too can give voice to their concerns. The Founder and Leader of the MQM [Altaf Hussain] lives in a small flat—no Pakistani politician lives in a house as small as mine. All of MQM's Central Cabinet, all the persons in charge of zones, all unit organizers, all those in charge of sectors and circles, every one of them lives in small houses or small flats. The reason for the opposition we are faced with is that the exploitative classes are afraid that all of Pakistan's poor might decide to follow in our footsteps.

I would like to ask the poor, the oppressed, the peasants and labourers, *haris* and small jobholders, 'Who are the exploiters in your region?' Look, they are the feudal landowners, the *waderas*, the capitalists, the *sardars*, and the Choudhries. Even though they are from your own nationality, see whether they love you? Do they solve your problems? How do they recompense you for your hard work? Think, who exploits you and how?

If you do not help yourself, do not expect help from anyone. Even God helps those who struggle for their own goals, as mentioned in *Surah Ar-Ra'd* of the Quran:

> Surely never
> Will Allah change the condition
> Of a people until they
> change it themselves
> (With their own souls). (13:11)

So I repeat, my poor, oppressed compatriots, struggle for your rights. Don't imagine Altaf Hussain or the MQM is your enemy. The MQM is a friend of the poor, whether they are from Punjab, Sindh, NWFP, or Balochistan. My brothers, don't believe the propaganda that says that Altaf Hussain is against the Punjabis, the Pakhtuns, or anybody else. We are against the exploiters only whether they are Punjabi, Pakhtun, Baloch, Sindhi, or Mohajir.

APPENDIX

Details of the Points in the Charter of Resolutions

1. Domicile Certificates and Identity Cards

It is obvious that, in the official and semi-official organizations of Sindh, even in the local, city organizations, there are a large number of employees and officers from outside Sindh. Many of them have obtained the Sindh domicile through various illegal means and, just by obtaining the domicile, they believe that they have a valid claim to Sindh's resources. The MQM considers such people 'Non-local individuals holding local domicile'. Similarly, numerous individuals have acquired Sindhi identity cards through legal or illegal means. Among them are people from outside Sindh as well as Afghans and other foreigners. Consequently, the rights of the local people of Sindh are undermined and fewer chances of employment are left open to them. Therefore:

- The Sindh domicile should be given solely to those people who have lived in Sindh for at least 20 years along with their families.
- To obtain a domicile certificate, it should be made mandatory to possess a certificate of permanent residence (PRC), a birth certificate, the matriculation certificate, and a testimonial certified by the elected Councillor of the region. However, an exception would be made in the case of those Pakistanis who were stranded in Bangladesh and have been brought to, and settled in, Sindh.
- The domicile certificates of all those people who do not belong to the 'local' category should be cancelled. Those who provide or obtain fake domicile certificates should be punished under the same law that is applied to cases of fake passport holders.

- A committee of Sindhi and Mohajir MPAs should be formed to investigate the authenticity of domicile certificates issued every year.
- The Sindh domicile should be made a mandatory requirement for obtaining an identity card in Sindh.

2. The Police

The local police are one of those government institutions through which people see themselves as participants in local administration. But the Sindh police, especially the police in Sindh's urban centres, consists of people who do not have links with Sindh. This alien profile of the Sindh police dates back to the time when Sindh was a part of the 'One Unit' and Karachi was the capital of the country. The rationale for the preponderance of non-locals in the Sindh police is said to be that the local people are not interested in joining the force while local people complain that the police department refuses to give them employment. Another explanation given is that the non-locals in the police are the same people who were recruited during 'One Unit' and the rest have Sindh's domicile. But the truth is that those who were recruited during One Unit should have retired by now while those who the police says are local domicile-holders are actually 'Non-local individuals holding local domicile'.

Thus, the actual situation today is that, not only does the Sindh police consist of non-locals, it continues to recruit non-local individuals on the pretext that the locals are not interested in joining the police force.

On the one hand, there is increased unemployment among local people on account of the non-local preponderance in the force and, on the other, the non-locals are unable to understand the temperament and the minds of the people of Sindh. These factors give rise to political and social confusion. Furthermore, the non-local police officers have no consideration for the citizens' and their welfare, for their social and economic problems, and for genuine maintenance of peace here.

The true role of the non-local police and their unsympathetic attitude towards local people became apparent in 1985 when, during riots in Karachi instigated by a conspiracy, the police was a party in the violence perpetrated on the local population. This has remained the pattern for, to this day, the police has played an active role in all the riots that have taken place. They are known to have massacred unarmed civilians and arrested innocent children as well as elderly and young people. On 14 and 15 December 1986, in the presence of this non-local police, Mohajirs were massacred in Qasba and Aligarh colonies, Orangi Town, and other townships. The carnage went on for six hours but the police took no action. It seemed as though history was replaying the tragedy of Jallianwala Bagh and the General Dyer of this massacre was sitting somewhere in the offices of the police department.

In the cities of Sindh, prejudice and hatred for the local population among the 'non-local police department' has increased to such an extent that the officers of the law never miss an opportunity to plunder the homes of local people. The police in Karachi especially, has itself actually been involved in thefts and robberies. The situation in the rural areas is almost as bad where the attitude of the non-local policemen towards the local population is tyrannical.

The non-local police is also responsible for the growth of the drug mafia, sale of firearms, and the increase in serious crimes. It is also involved in the growth of land-grabbing because without, the involvement of the police, so many illegal settlements could not have come up. The root cause of the whole situation is that there are in the Sindh police many non-local individuals who have no interest in the law and order, welfare, and prosperity of this province. The reason for this is that they have not come here to settle down but to stay for some time and make money. Therefore:

- In all parts of Sindh, including Karachi, only members of the local population should be recruited in the police department as well as all related agencies and institutions from the lowest cadre to the highest.
- From the highest office of the Sindh police to the lowest, non-local employees should be replaced by local individuals and the non-local officers and workers currently working here

should be transferred back to the police department in their own provinces.

- A separate police force consisting of local individuals should be created for the local Municipal institutions whose main job it should be to stop illegal activities, liberate land from land grabbers, and create respect for municipal laws.

3. Instituting a Scheme of Issuing Licenses for Weapons

In the last few years, traders in drugs and illegal weapons and enemies of Mohajirs have killed hundreds of Mohajirs and maimed thousands of them in the cities of Sindh. In these attacks, the police not only failed to provide security to the innocent Mohajir victims but also actually helped the assailants in several cases. Those who attacked Mohajir settlements were never arrested nor were their modern automatic weapons seized from any of them. Armed attacks on Mohajir settlements have become a daily routine. It is a situation in which Mohajirs feel extremely insecure and they want to be able to defend themselves and their property. A similar environment of insecurity prevails in rural Sindh and in the old Baloch settlements of Sindh. Therefore:

- Mohajirs and Sindhis should be issued licences for weapons.
- To issue licenses for weapons, the same simple procedure should be used which is already being used in the case of radio and television licences.

4. Relocation of Afghan Refugees

Heroin, Kalashnikovs, and illegal modern automatic weapons have become common among many of the Afghan refugees after their arrival in Sindh. Their presence in large numbers in the cities of Sindh, especially Karachi, and their involvement in the city and its business life, are a rejection of the policy under which refugees should be confined to their camps. Because of this, the crime rate has risen alarmingly in the cities of Sindh. Therefore:

- Afghan refugees should be confined to camps near the Afghan border.
- They should be stopped from interfering in the life of the cities, buying property, and starting businesses.

5. Unnatural Increase in Population

It is an acknowledged fact that, in the urban areas of Sindh, especially in Karachi, the population is growing at a phenomenal rate. The rate of growth in population is 6 per cent in Karachi while, in other urban areas of the country, it is 3 per cent. Such a rapid increase in population is unlawful and unnatural. The reason for this abnormal increase is the unchecked arrival of individuals from the other provinces. It is the cause of extraordinary strain on the resources of Sindh and is also giving rise to social and racial biases and discrimination.

Illegal arrivals from other provinces are, on the one hand, a burden on Sindh's resources and, on the other, they make no contribution to Sindh's tax revenues. One example of this is that the special development programme for Karachi will cost the city an extra 2,040,000,000 rupees. Such special development programmes have been started in Balochistan, the tribal areas, and in the rain-irrigated agricultural lands of Punjab as well though there it is the indigenous population that is benefiting from them and also financing them with their taxes. However, in Sindh, these programmes benefit mostly the non-local population since development works such as the building of roads, etc. will, by and large, take place in the illegal settlements. A fourth of the total amount of the development funds will be spent on developing the illicit settlements where most of the population comprises illegal arrivals. It should be born in mind that, after all, the establishment of these settlements is itself illegal. On the other hand, these programmes are financed by the taxpayers who are the local inhabitants of Sindh.

Everybody knows the disadvantages of an abnormally large increase in population and it is also a fact that the resources of Sindh can no longer sustain such an upsurge of people. This fact has been acknowledged not only by former Prime Minister, Mohammad Khan

Junejo, and the President, General Mohammad Ziaul Haq, but also by most political leaders. Therefore:

- To stop the unnatural growth in Sindh's population, people coming here from other provinces of Pakistan should be given jobs and business opportunities in their own provinces.
- With the help of the media, the Government of Sindh should start a campaign to convince the people of other provinces that Sindh's sources of income are now limited to the extent that, even in the private sector, there are not enough funds for investment. Therefore, Sindh can no longer be burdened with more people.
- High officials and political and social leaders in the other provinces should be requested to try to increase means of livelihood in their own provinces so that the people there are not forced to leave behind their families and travel hundreds of miles in pursuit of livelihoods.

6. Illegal Land-Grabbing and Illegal Settlements

Illegal land-grabbing goes on constantly in the urban and rural areas of Sindh. Land-grabbers keep annexing more and more land and create illegal settlements. Such illegal acquisition of land has become a lucrative business in Sindh and is run mostly by organized groups of non-local individuals. This shows that illegal acquisition of land is by no means linked to poverty.

The organized group which is involved in the business of acquiring land through illegal means annexes land wherever it wants to making a travesty of state laws. These organized groups work with complete freedom not only because they consider themselves above the law but also because the law enforcing agencies do not interfere with their activities and are even known to help them after getting a share in their profits.

In no other part of the country has the writ of the provincial government been challenged on such a scale. Land-grabbing has become easier in Sindh because those who are involved in this business are non-local individuals and those responsible for enforcing the law also come from outside Sindh.

In 1978, the President of Pakistan announced that all illegal settlements established before 1978 would be legalized. This announcement indicated that the illegal act of grabbing land had been granted legal protection and is bound to encourage the land-grabbers. Indeed, as a result of the announcement hundreds of new illegal settlements surfaced in the cities of Sindh. Seven years later, in March 1985, there was another announcement, this time, by the former Prime Minister, Mohammad Khan Junejo, who declared that all the settlements built before 1985 would be regularized.

These announcements and their consequences have proved that legalizing illegal settlements is a boost to land-grabbing. It becomes even more vigorous after such announcements. In other words, it seems the government adopts a defensive role in dealing with land-grabbing and, as a result, the owners of this contemptible business become bolder.

This whole state of affairs gives the impression that the Government of Sindh has acknowledged the right of every new non-local arrival in Sindh to one (illegal) plot of land and one reason for the growing pressure of the non-local population in Sindh is this encouragement from the government. Therefore:

- Only those illegal settlements that were built in Sindh before 1978 should be legalized.
- The act of land-grabbing should be declared a cognizable offence.
- A suitable law should be made for punishing anyone involved in this business and the SHO in charge of that area should be made responsible for it.
- The practice of allotting land in Sindh as rewards or grants to non-local individuals should be stopped. Sindh's agricultural land should be allotted only to the locals of Sindh.

7. Transport

In the cities of Sindh, especially in Karachi, private transport is controlled by mostly uneducated people. Most of the drivers in this transport system are also uneducated. Their driving skills do not come up to the required standard, but they have managed to obtain their driving license through illegal means. They are known for fast and reckless driving, overtaking other vehicles from the wrong lane, breaking traffic rules, and being rude to all passengers including women and children. The traffic police avoid taking steps against them because many of the vehicles are owned by high police or administration officers. Besides, monthly funds, provided as bribes by the transport owners to the traffic police, hinder the officers from taking proper action against offenders. For these reasons, Karachi has a high average of traffic accidents. According to one report, 37.5 per cent of the traffic accidents every year and two deaths per day involve buses and minibuses.

Six thousand buses and mini buses ply the roads of Karachi but, because of the large population, even this number is insufficient to solve the transport problem in the city. Thus transport is a serious problem for the people of Karachi.

Furthermore, Karachi's roads are now too narrow for the growing traffic in the city. Similarly, the highways connecting the different cities of Sindh are insufficient for the burgeoning traffic and are the scene of many accidents. Therefore:

- A fast, modern traffic system (e.g. the electric train) should be introduced in the urban and rural areas of Sindh, including Karachi and Hyderabad, as is done in other developing countries.
- In the cities of Sindh, government transport should be made the responsibility of the Municipal authority.
- Education up to Matriculation level should be made a requirement for the issuing of a driver's licencse to those who seek to drive a public transport vehicle. Computers should be used to test drivers for issuing licenses.

- Illiterate people should, under no condition, be issued professional driving licenses, and preference should be given to local people in the issuing of professional licenses.
- Flyovers should be constructed over the important roads and crossings of Karachi.
- Traffic rules should be firmly implemented.
- Roads connecting the cities of Sindh should be broadened.
- To solve the parking problem in the city, parking lots should be made near the more crowded and important business centres of the cities.
- There should be discounted fares for students travelling between the cities of Sindh.
- Loading trucks and tankers carrying heavy loads should not be allowed to enter Karachi. A ring road should be built to take them directly from the port and the industrial area to the Super Highway and the National Highway thereby bypassing the city.

8. Unemployment

The proportion of 15 to 29-year-olds to the total population is far higher in Sindh than in the other provinces. Unemployment is, therefore, also higher. Besides, people coming from the other provinces look for jobs here making the situation worse. These non-local people easily find jobs in Sindh, because they are helped by the non-locals who have high positions in government and semi-government organizations, corporations, industry, banks, police and other departments. This kind of patronage goes against the interests of the local population.

The following is an example of this: According to a report in 1987, 45 per cent of government officers working in Sindh's police or administration do not have a Sindh domicile. Among CSS and CSP officers of grades 18 to 21, 36 possess Sindh domicile, 24 posses Punjab domicile, 4 have domiciles of the NWFP, and 1 possesses Balochistan domicile (*Daily News*, 24 October 1987).

This situation has made the unemployment issue extremely serious, complicated, and painful. Therefore:

- Local persons from Sindh should be given preference for employment in all government and semi-government organizations and, corporations from the lowest to the highest levels of administration. Non-locals who are currently serving in those positions should be accommodated in their own provinces.
- In positions where the incumbent provides various facilities (such as tender, license, quota, NOCs for establishing industries, etc.) for business, trade, and industry, local persons should be given preference in employment.
- In the purely local organizations of Sindh, only local persons should be employed.

9. The Right to Vote

Hundreds of thousands of non-local people in Sindh are registered as voters in Sindh as well as in their native province. This gives them the right to vote in both places. Not only is this irregular, it also provides the non-locals with a double advantage to which citizens are not entitled. By using their voting right in Sindh these individuals choose their representative in Sindh as well. The representative then obtains development funds from the resources of Sindh even though the non-locals who voted him into that position make no contribution to Sindh's resources. As a consequence, the local population of Sindh is deprived of its rights.

Moreover, when such a large number of people have left their own provinces and regions, then, for those provinces and regions, there should be a proportionate reduction in the number of Assembly seats and an increase in Sindh's seats in the National Assembly. But this does not happen. Therefore:

- Nobody should be allowed to vote in Sindh except the local people.

10. The Age of the Voter

In the Constitution framed by the elected government in 1973 it was stated that, whenever the next general elections were held, the minimum age of voters would be reduced from 21 to 18 years but this did not happen and, consequently, a large number of the country's young people were deprived of their vote. Therefore:

• In future the minimum voting age for the municipal, provincial, and national elections should be fixed at 18 years in accordance with the 1973 Constitution.

11. The Quota System

In Pakistan today, Sindh is the only province in which the Sindh Assembly passed the Pakistan Resolution. The Muslims of Sindh warmly welcomed the Muslims who migrated to Pakistan from the Muslim-minority provinces of India. For this act of generosity the Mohajirs are indebted to the Sindhis and would like to maintain a brotherly relationship with them.

The Mohajirs brought with them political awareness, skills, and the capacity for practical work. They contributed immensely to Sindh's progress. A few years after the creation of Pakistan, however, the exploitative forces devised 'One Unit' that was primarily to get greater control of the resources and economy of East Pakistan and the effects of this measure were visible in Sindh as well. One example of this is that, even after the end of the 'One Unit', Sindh was saddled with 17,000 non-local employees who, instead of being sent back to their respective provinces, remained in Sindh.

Efforts were made to crush the Mohajirs as well who possessed political strength and insight and were capable of confronting exploitative elements. In addition, various attempts were made to create distance and hostility between Mohajirs and Sindhis. The first attempt of this kind was made during the rule of Ayub Khan when the teaching of the Sindhi language was discontinued in schools and Urdu was made compulsory for Sindhi students as well. Later, during Mr Zulfikar Ali Bhutto's days, not only was dissension created with the introduction of urban and rural quotas but also clashes over language were fanned. The third such attempt was made by General Ziaul Haq who, with a stroke of the pen, extended the quota system by ten years when the true representatives of Sindhis had made no such demand. In this period, the exploitative elements had taken full control of Sindh. Their aim was to see Mohajirs and Sindhis become bitter enemies and remain in conflict so that they could continue to hold Sindh in their talons. This is why some of them are still supporting the quota system hoping to incite the Sindhis against the Mohajirs while others are opposing it in order to incite the Mohajirs against the Sindhis although neither of the two groups raising these issues have anything remotely to do with the quota system.

The MQM's stand on this issue is that we should be discreet as well as realistic. Mohajirs are in the majority in Sindh's urban areas while Sindhis predominate in the rural areas. What needs to be noted is that, to boost the rural areas of Punjab economically and bring them closer to the level in the urban areas, special funds have been allocated. On the other hand, in Sindh, for the same goal, the quota system was introduced!

In this situation, it would not be incorrect to say that the quota system is indirectly a strong proof of the separate nationality and position of the Mohajirs. However, the MQM considers the quota system that is currently in force in Sindh to be utterly unjust and a contemptible tool of the exploitative forces. The MQM's stand is that the present quota system should be revised and based on the basis of the Mohajir and Sindhi populations.

Moreover, Sindh is not being given its full share of the federal quota for the provinces because this quota is not being divided as it was supposed to be. Therefore:

- An accurate census count should be held of the Sindhi and Mohajir populations. On the basis of the proportion between the Sindhi and Mohajir populations emerging from this census, they should be given responsible positions in government jobs and educational institutions. Mohajirs and Sindhis should be given admission to the technical institutes in Sindh also on the basis of the proportion of their populations.

- A committee consisting of selected Mohajir and Sindhi representatives should be made to implement the quota system in a just way.
- The 10 per cent quota for merit in employment on the federal level should be abolished and the share should be distributed among federal units on the basis of their population.
- Jobs at the federal level, whether in Administration or Defence, should also be given to each province in proportion to population.
- Sindh should be given its full and rightful quota at the federal level in proportion to the population of the province. This should be done and implemented in a transparent and honest way.

12. Employment in Industrial Organizations

It is a sorry situation that local people are not provided employment in the industrial organizations of Sindh leading to an increasing sense of deprivation and unemployment among the local population. At the same time, the golden opportunities for employment in these organizations available to non-local people are drawing more non-locals to Sindh. This practice is so widespread that in the newly-discovered oilfields of Sindh, local labourers and skilled workers are not given jobs.

Furthermore, in the private sector in Sindh, labourers are hired through contractors. These contractors are non-locals and prefer to induct non-local labourers. Moreover, the contractors take away a part of the labourers' income without putting in any work themselves. Therefore:

- In all of Sindh's government and private organizations, local labour should be given preference. Non-local skilled workers should be given jobs only if local skilled workers are not available.
- A law should be passed to abolish the contractor system of hiring workers. A law should be enacted to make the contractor system illegal.

13. Injustice to Mohajirs in
Various Organizations

Starting with Ayub Khan and until now, every government has sent a large number of Mohajir high officials into forced retirement on some pretext or accusation. Such actions have left Mohajirs with a deep sense of deprivation and a feeling of being denied participation in the administrative matters of the country. In addition, like former governments, various government and semi-government organizations and corporations even today have permanent policies which not only hurt the Mohajirs but also deprive them of jobs. For example, the present government has made a rule that retires people after 25 years of work in PIA. As a matter of principle, this law should affect only those people who were taken on when or after the law was passed. But, purely on the basis of enmity towards Mohajirs, the law was applied to Mohajirs who had been working for PIA for the preceding 25 years and had played an important role in the growth and development of PIA. Therefore:

- The same rules should be made for all federal and provincial government and semi-government organizations and corporations; the employees who were forcibly retired by their organizations under these 'special' laws should be compensated for the period of employment they were deprived of by being forced to retire.
- All policies of government and semi-government organizations and corporations which directly hurt Mohajirs should be done away with forthwith.
- Weeding out Mohajirs by various organizations should be stopped immediately.

14. Bringing the Mohajirs in
Bangladesh to Pakistan

The people who are known as the Mohajirs of East Pakistan are those non-Bengali Pakistanis who had migrated to East Pakistan at the time of Partition. In the war of 1971, they made great sacrifices for Pakistan. But, after the fall of East Pakistan, only a few of them were brought to Pakistan while the greater number of them are still languishing in the Red Cross camps of Bangladesh, seventeen years after the split. Whatever the law under which the few were brought to Pakistan, the fact is that those who are left behind are part of the same people, and it is not known under which law these others are not being brought here.

According to the Charter of the United Nations, when a country is divided, its inhabitants have a fundamental right to choose to be the citizens of either part. In modern history, the partition of the subcontinent offers an example of the application of this rule. At the time of Partition, the people of the subcontinent were given the right to choose between the citizenship of India or Pakistan.

The Pakistanis stranded in Bangladesh had opted, not for Bangladesh, but for Pakistan and had fought for Pakistan until East Pakistan fell. Besides, after the fall of Dhaka in 1971 not only did they express their desire to come to Pakistan but also, believe themselves to be Pakistani and still call themselves Pakistani which is why they have every right to come to Pakistan and this basic right cannot be denied them.

Funds have been collected on the international level to bring stranded Pakistanis from Bangladesh to Pakistan and to settle them in the country. This is perhaps the only example in the whole world of a state refusing to accept the citizenship of its own people. The government of Pakistan should learn from the example of the United States. The US brought back even the Vietnamese who were loyal to it recognizing their right to US citizenship. Therefore:

- The Pakistani citizenship of Pakistanis stranded in Bangladesh should be recognized and arrangements should be made to bring them here forthwith.

15. The Khokhrapar Route and Postal Rates

To open the Khokhrapar route is an old demand of the Mohajirs and Sindhis who want to travel to India. Former Prime Minister Mohammad Khan Junejo had announced during a meeting in Nishtar

Park that the route would be opened, but no steps were taken to implement this announcement. If this route is opened, Mohajirs and Sindhis travelling to India will be able to save both money and time which are precious to all. Moreover, the currently prevailing postal and telegraph rates between Pakistan and India are higher than those in any of Pakistan's neighbouring countries. Therefore:

- The Khokhrapar route should be opened forthwith in accordance with the demands of Sindhis and Mohajirs as already announced by the government.
- Pakistan should have the same telegraph and postal rates as those prevailing in its neighbouring countries.

16. Educational Institutions

Generally, it is the local students of a place who are given preference in the matter of admissions to educational institutions. But, in the educational institutions of Sindh, especially the institutions for technical education, the conditions are different. There are even such institutions where admission of local students is ignored altogether.

The literacy rate in Sindh is much higher than that in the other regions of Pakistan except Hunza. However, because of the shortage of educational institutions in Sindh, thousands of children and older students are denied admission in schools and colleges and are thus deprived of education. The basic reason for this is that no new educational institutions are being established here by the government. Besides, the government does not give extra funds to the existing educational institutions so that they may enhance their capacity and accommodate more students. Therefore:

- Local students should be given preference in admission to Sindh's educational institutions and only those non-local students should be accommodated there who are the children of federal employees posted in Sindh.

- The female students of Karachi should be admitted to medical colleges in Karachi and should not be compelled to apply for admission in medical colleges located in interior Sindh.
- The grants to Sindh's universities and other educational institutions should be increased. The amount of the grant should be in proportion to the number of students in the institution.
- The number of schools, colleges, universities, technical schools, and institutions for teaching professional skills in Sindh should be increased in accordance with the increasing literacy rate.
- At least one more university and one other medical college should be established in Karachi without delay.
- Sindh's educational budget should be increased in proportion to the increasing literacy rate in the province.

17. Health

Most of the people of Sindh are even now deprived of health facilities. The number of government hospitals in Sindh is extremely small compared to the size of Sindh's population. In the existing hospitals, there is a great shortage of medicines and other facilities. On the other hand, the expenses of private hospitals are beyond the means of a common citizen. Because of this situation, the proportion of sick people is rising. Moreover, Karachi's Sindh Medical College is the only medical college in Pakistan that does not have a hospital attached to it. The Jinnah Postgraduate Medical Centre is a federal institution where doctors from the whole country are given employment on the basis of the quota system. Because of this situation, a large number of students who graduate from Sindh Medical College are deprived of house jobs and not only do they not get the necessary experience, but they are also not able to fulfil the requirement of working in a recognized hospital which is a basic condition for further, higher professional education. Therefore:

- There should be a suitable increase in the health budget of Sindh.

- The condition of the existing hospitals should be improved, and, wherever possible, the premises should be expanded to accommodate more beds.
- A separate hospital attached to the Sindh Medical College should be established or Jinnah Hospital should be attached to Sindh Medical College and handed over to the Government of Sindh.

18. Residential Facilities

A large number of Sindh's urban and rural dwellers do not own a home. Often, in the cities, there are crowded areas where several families live together in a single, small house. Like the Sindhis and the Mohajirs, in many places in Sindh including Karachi, old Baloch, Makrani, and Kachhi families are still living in settlements which are devoid of the basic amenities of life. These people should be given their rights and, for that, it is necessary to do the following:

- Under a special scheme, all those families in the local population who have no private accommodation or do not have the means to buy or build a home, should be provided a plot of land each at a special, low price and a loan to construct a house on easy terms.

19. KESC

This corporation used to work under the Sindh Government but, a few years back, it was handed over to WAPDA without any cogent reason. KESC's merger with WAPDA not only deprived hundreds of local people of their jobs and opened new opportunities for non-local people, but also, at the same time, its performance was greatly affected. Therefore:

- KESC should be separated from WAPDA and restored to its earlier position. The non-local employees of KESC should be removed and their services transferred to WAPDA.

20. Sales Tax

The government of Sindh is short of funds for its development programmes. It has to either approach the federal government repeatedly for funds or take loans from international financial institutions. This happens despite the fact that Sindh pays the federal government more tax than any of the other provinces. Therefore:

• The Sindh Government should be given the right to collect sales tax.

21. Public Holidays

Hazrat Shah Abdul Latif Bhitai was a famous Sindhi Sufi and a great and widely known poet who taught the world lessons of love and peace. Not just the people of Sindh but those in other parts of Pakistan feel a deep reverence and affection for him because he devoted his life to the service and love of humanity.

Liaquat Ali Khan was a leader of the first rank in the Pakistan Movement and Pakistan's first Prime Minister. He left behind in India all the luxuries of a *nawab's* life and migrated to Pakistan empty handed. Liaquat Ali Khan was a national hero. When he was killed in a public meeting in Rawalpindi, his last words were for Pakistan. Therefore:

• Keeping in view the feelings of the people of Pakistan and specifically, of Sindh, and the services of Shah Latif and Liaquat Ali Khan, these two great people should be remembered on a national level. Shah Latif's death anniversary and Liaquat Ali Khan's day of martyrdom should be declared public holidays throughout the country.

Glossary

Allah-o-Akbar	'God is great', an Arabic phrase which is used in the Muslim prayers as well as in the call to prayers. It is also quite frequently used by Muslims in ordinary speech, especially as an exclamation.
Desh	One's native land, as in Bangladesh, land of the Bengalis.
dupatta	A sort of scarf worn by subcontinental women, but more often Pakistani women over *kameez* and *shalwar*. Often used to cover the head though its main object is to drape over the bosom.
Eid	Muslim festival. There is one Eid celebrating the completion of fasting in the month of Ramzan, and another celebrating the completion of the Haj.
Eidi	Eid gift in the form of cash.
Fateha Khawani	An occasion on which the *fateha* (see below) is recited for the dead by a group of people.
Fateha	The first chapter of the Quran. It is recited as a prayer for the dead, an occasion or act known by the same name. It is also recited when distributing food among the poor as well as among one's own friends and relatives as a pious offering to God.
fatwas	A verdict based on Islamic religious law.
Haq Parast	Literally, 'those who worship the truth'. A part of the Pakistani political party, MQM, headed by Altaf Hussain.

haris	Crop-sharing tenants.
hijrat	Literally, migration. Since the Prophet (PBUH) and his Companions' migration from Makkah to Medina, it has been used for migration with a noble or religious cause as the migration of Muslims from India to the 'Muslim homeland' of Pakistan.
Isha prayers	The last of the five daily and obligatory Muslim prayers, said at night.
Islami Jamiat-e-Tulba (IJT)	An ultra right students' wing of Jamaat-e-Islami (JI).
Islami Nizam	Islamic system of governance.
Jamiat	Union or organization
Jeeay Mohajir	Literally, 'Long live the Mohajir' (one who has migrated—see 'hijrat') A slogan of Altaf Hussain's party, the MQM.
kababs	Barbequed or fried mincemeat with spices either in the shape of patties or sausages.
kameez	Pakistani version of a shirt.
Khatam-e Nabuwat	The end of the process and routine of appointing Prophets and Messengers by Almighty Allah. None will be appointed as a prophet after Hazrat Muhammad (PBUH). Muhammad is the Last of the Prophets.
Maaf karo	Literally 'Forgive me'. A term usually used to refuse a beggar.
Mian	Honorific, attached to the name of a man.
Mohajirs	Immigrants. In Pakistan this term has come to be associated with people who migrated from India at the time of the partition of the subcontinent in 1947.
Mufti	A Sunni Islamic scholar who is an interpreter or expounder of Islamic law (Sharia).

Mukti Bahini	Literally, 'Liberation Army'. Armed fighters of East Bengal who fought the Pakistan army after the proclamation of Bangladesh's independence.
Nara-e-Mohajir	Literally, 'The slogan of the Mohajir'.
Nara-e-Takbir	A term meaning 'Allah-o-Akbar' used as a cry or slogan.
Nazim	Literally, manager or administrator. An Urdu word for an elected officer who is the administrative head of a district or like the mayor of a city.
nihari	A kind of slow-cooked, spicy beef stew.
Nizam-i-Mustafa	Literally, 'Muhammad's System'. Commonly understood as the Islamic system of governance as practised by Prophet Muhammad (PBUH).
parathas	Unleavened flatbread made from wheat flour, spread with *ghee* (clarified butter) re-folded and rolled out a second time, before shallow frying.
Pir	A holy man with followers.
pitthu parade	Routine punishment drill.
Quami	National
qorma	Meat curry.
Quaid-i-Azam	Great Leader. The title given to the founder of Pakistan Mohammad Ali Jinnah.
rajwaras	Principalities.
samosa	Deep fried triangular pastry, usually with a spiced mincemeat and potato filling.
subedar major	Senior rank of junior commissioned officer in the Pakistan army.
waderas	Landlords who own large portions of land in rural Sindh.

Index